W9-BFE-802

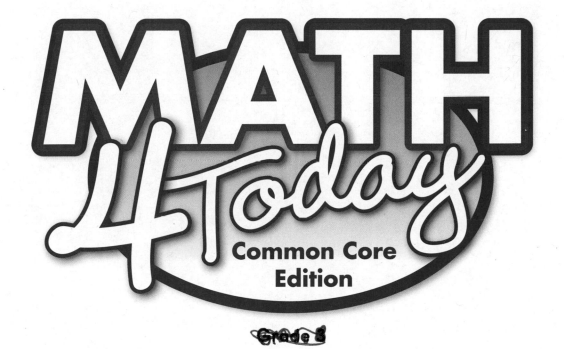

# MATH 4 Today

## Common Core Edition

Grade 3

Erin McCarthy

Carson-Dellosa Publishing, LLC
Greensboro, North Carolina

A a a a B b B c c D d E e F f g G

H h I i j J k k L L m M N O o P P Q q

R r s S H T U u U v V w W x X

Y y z Z

## Credits

Content Editor: Elise Craver
Copy Editor: Karen Seberg

Carson-Dellosa Publishing, LLC
PO Box 35665
Greensboro, NC 27425 USA
carsondellosa.com

© 2013, Carson-Dellosa Publishing, LLC. The purchase of this material entitles the buyer to reproduce worksheets and activities for classroom use only—not for commercial resale. Reproduction of these materials for an entire school or district is prohibited. No part of this book may be reproduced (except as noted above), stored in a retrieval system, or transmitted in any form or by any means (mechanically, electronically, recording, etc.) without the prior written consent of Carson-Dellosa Publishing, LLC.

Printed in the USA • All rights reserved.

ISBN 978-1-62442-601-8
13-134181151

# Table of Contents

# Introduction

*Common Core Math 4 Today: Daily Skill Practice* is a perfect supplement to any classroom math curriculum. Students' math skills will grow as they work on numbers, operations, algebraic thinking, place value, measurement, data, and geometry.

This book covers 40 weeks of daily practice. Four math problems a day for four days a week will provide students with ample practice in math skills. A separate assessment of 10 questions is included for the fifth day of each week.

Various skills and concepts are reinforced throughout the book through activities that align to the Common Core State Standards. To view these standards, please see the Common Core State Standards Alignment Matrix on pages 7 and 8.

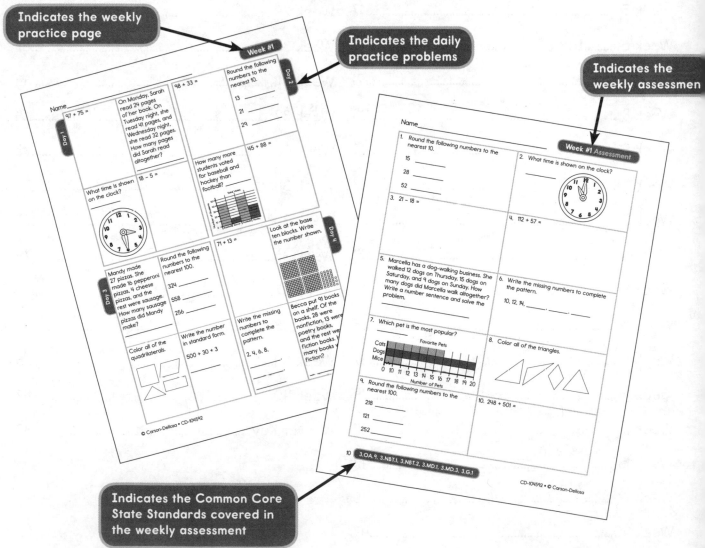

Indicates the weekly practice page

Indicates the daily practice problems

Indicates the weekly assessmen

Indicates the Common Core State Standards covered in the weekly assessment

CD-104592 • © Carson-Dellosa

The daily practice problems and weekly assessments in *Common Core Math 4 Today: Daily Skill Practice* help students achieve proficiency with the grade-level Common Core State Standards. Throughout the year, students should also work on building their comfort with the Standards for Mathematical Practice. Use the following suggestions to extend the problems in *Common Core Math 4 Today: Daily Skill Practice*.

1. **Make sense of problems and persevere in solving them.**

   Students should make sure that they understand a problem before trying to solve it. After solving, students should check their answers, often just by asking themselves if their answers make sense in the context of the question. Incorporate the following ideas into your Math 4 Today time:

   • Encourage students to underline the important parts of word problems and to draw lines through any extra information.
   • Allow students to talk through their answers with partners and explain why they think their answers make sense.

2. **Reason abstractly and quantitatively.**

   Students should be able to represent problems with numbers and symbols without losing the original meaning of the numbers and the symbols. A student who is successful at this practice will be able to reason about questions related to the original problem and use flexibility in solving problems. Incorporate the following ideas into your Math 4 Today time:

   • Ask students questions to extend the problems. For example, if a problem asks students to evenly divide a set of 10, ask them to describe what they would do if the set increased to 11.
   • Have students choose a computation problem and write a word problem to accompany it.

3. **Construct viable arguments and critique the reasoning of others.**

   Students should understand mathematical concepts well enough to be able to reason about and prove or disprove answers. As students become more comfortable with mathematical language, they should use math talk to explain their thinking. Incorporate the following ideas into your Math 4 Today time:

   • Have students work with partners and use mathematical language to explain their ways of thinking about a problem.
   • Encourage students to use manipulatives and drawings to support their reasoning.

4. **Model with mathematics.**

   Students should apply their mathematical knowledge to situations in the real world. They can use drawings, graphs, charts, and other tools to make sense of situations, as well as use skills such as estimation to approach a problem before solving it. Incorporate the following ideas into your Math 4 Today time:

# Incorporating the Standards for Mathematical Practice

- Encourage students to take a problem they have solved and explain how it could help them solve a problem in their own lives.
- Ask students to identify tools, such as charts or graphs, that could help them solve a problem.

5. **Use appropriate tools strategically.**

Students should be able to use a range of tools to help them solve problems, as well as make decisions about which tools to use in different situations. Proficient students will use skills such as estimation to evaluate if the tools helped them solve the problem correctly. Incorporate the following ideas into your Math 4 Today time:

- Ask students to discuss which tools would be most and least helpful in solving a problem.
- As a class, discuss how two students using the same tool could have arrived at the same answer. Encourage students to identify the errors and the limitations in using certain tools.

6. **Attend to precision.**

Students should be thorough in their use of mathematical symbols and labels. They should understand that without them, and without understanding their meanings, math problems are not as meaningful. Incorporate the following ideas into your Math 4 Today time:

- Ask students to explain how a problem or an answer would change if a label on a graph were changed.
- Have students go on a scavenger hunt for the week to identify units of measure in the problems, operations symbols, or graph labels.

7. **Look for and make use of structure.**

Students identify and use patterns to help them extend their knowledge to new concepts. Understanding patterns and structure will also help students be flexible in their approaches to solving problems. Incorporate the following ideas into your Math 4 Today time:

- Have students become pattern detectives and look for any patterns in each week's problems.
- Ask students to substitute a different set of numbers into a problem and see if any patterns emerge.

8. **Look for and express regularity in repeated reasoning.**

Students are able to use any patterns they notice to find shortcuts that help them solve other problems. They can observe a problem with an eye toward finding repetition, instead of straight computation. Incorporate the following ideas into your Math 4 Today time:

- Allow students to share any shortcuts they may find during their problem solving. As a class, try to understand why the shortcuts work.
- When students find patterns, have them explain how the patterns could help them solve other problems.

© Copyright 2010. National Governors Association Center for Best Practices and Council of Chief State School Officers. All rights reserved.

CD-104592 • © Carson-Dellosa

| STANDARD | W1 | W2 | W3 | W4 | W5 | W6 | W7 | W8 | W9 | W10 | W11 | W12 | W13 | W14 | W15 | W16 | W17 | W18 | W19 | W20 |
|---|---|---|---|---|---|---|---|---|---|---|---|---|---|---|---|---|---|---|---|---|
| 3.OA.1 | ● |  | ● |  | ● |  |  |  |  |  | ● |  | ● |  | ● |  | ● | ● | ● |  |
| 3.OA.2 |  |  |  |  |  |  |  |  |  |  |  |  |  |  |  | ● | ● | ● | ● |  |
| 3.OA.3 |  |  |  |  |  | ● | ● |  |  |  | ● | ● | ● | ● | ● | ● | ● | ● | ● | ● |
| 3.OA.4 |  |  |  |  |  |  |  |  |  | ● | ● | ● | ● | ● | ● | ● | ● | ● | ● | ● |
| 3.OA.5 |  |  |  |  |  |  |  |  |  |  | ● | ● | ● | ● | ● | ● | ● | ● | ● | ● |
| 3.OA.6 |  |  |  |  |  |  |  |  |  |  |  |  |  |  |  | ● | ● |  | ● | ● |
| 3.OA.7 |  |  |  |  |  |  |  |  |  |  | ● | ● | ● | ● | ● | ● | ● | ● | ● | ● |
| 3.OA.8 | ● | ● | ● | ● | ● |  | ● | ● | ● | ● |  | ● | ● | ● | ● | ● | ● | ● | ● | ● |
| 3.OA.9 | ● | ● | ● | ● | ● | ● | ● | ● | ● | ● | ● | ● | ● | ● | ● | ● | ● | ● | ● | ● |
| 3.NBT.1 | ● | ● | ● | ● | ● | ● | ● | ● | ● | ● | ● | ● | ● | ● | ● | ● | ● | ● | ● | ● |
| 3.NBT.2 | ● | ● | ● | ● | ● | ● | ● | ● | ● | ● | ● | ● | ● | ● | ● | ● | ● | ● | ● | ● |
| 3.NBT.3 |  |  |  |  |  |  |  |  |  |  | ● | ● | ● | ● | ● | ● | ● | ● | ● | ● |
| 3.NF.1 |  |  | ● |  |  |  |  |  |  |  |  |  |  |  |  |  |  |  |  |  |
| 3.NF.2a |  |  |  |  | ● |  |  |  |  |  |  |  |  |  |  |  |  |  |  |  |
| 3.NF.2b |  |  |  |  |  |  |  |  |  |  |  |  |  |  |  |  |  |  | ● |  |
| 3.NF.3a |  |  |  |  |  | ● |  |  |  | ● | ● |  |  |  | ● |  | ● |  |  |  |
| 3.NF.3b |  |  |  |  |  |  |  |  |  |  |  |  |  |  |  | ● |  |  |  |  |
| 3.NF.3c |  |  |  |  |  |  |  |  |  |  |  |  |  |  |  |  |  |  |  |  |
| 3.NF.3d |  |  |  |  | ● |  | ● |  | ● |  |  |  | ● |  | ● |  | ● |  |  |  |
| 3.MD.1 | ● | ● | ● | ● | ● | ● | ● | ● | ● | ● | ● | ● | ● | ● | ● | ● | ● | ● | ● |  |
| 3.MD.2 |  |  |  |  |  |  |  |  |  |  |  |  |  |  |  |  |  |  |  |  |
| 3.MD.3 | ● | ● | ● | ● | ● | ● | ● | ● | ● | ● |  | ● |  | ● |  |  |  |  | ● |  |
| 3.MD.4 |  |  |  |  |  |  |  |  |  |  |  |  |  |  |  |  |  |  |  |  |
| 3.MD.5a |  |  |  |  |  |  |  |  |  |  |  |  |  |  |  |  |  |  |  |  |
| 3.MD.5b |  |  |  |  |  |  |  |  |  |  |  |  |  |  |  |  |  |  |  |  |
| 3.MD.6 |  |  |  |  |  |  |  |  |  |  |  |  |  |  |  |  |  |  |  |  |
| 3.MD.7a |  |  |  |  |  |  |  |  |  |  |  |  |  |  |  |  |  |  |  |  |
| 3.MD.7b |  |  |  |  |  |  |  |  |  |  |  |  |  |  |  |  |  |  |  |  |
| 3.MD.7c |  |  |  |  |  |  |  |  |  |  |  |  |  |  |  |  |  |  |  |  |
| 3.MD.7d |  |  |  |  |  |  |  |  |  |  |  |  |  |  |  |  |  |  |  |  |
| 3.MD.8 |  |  |  |  |  |  |  |  |  |  |  |  |  |  |  |  |  |  |  |  |
| 3.G.1 | ● | ● | ● | ● | ● | ● | ● | ● | ● | ● | ● |  |  |  | ● |  |  |  |  |  |
| 3.G.2 |  |  |  |  |  |  |  |  |  |  |  |  |  |  |  |  |  |  |  |  |

W = Week

© Carson-Dellosa • CD-104592

| STANDARD | W21 | W22 | W23 | W24 | W25 | W26 | W27 | W28 | W29 | W30 | W31 | W32 | W33 | W34 | W35 | W36 | W37 | W38 | W39 | W40 |
|---|---|---|---|---|---|---|---|---|---|---|---|---|---|---|---|---|---|---|---|---|
| 3.OA.1 |  | ● |  | ● |  |  |  |  |  |  |  |  |  |  |  |  |  |  |  |  |
| 3.OA.2 |  | ● |  |  |  |  |  |  |  |  |  |  |  |  |  |  |  |  |  |  |
| 3.OA.3 | ● |  | ● | ● | ● | ● | ● | ● | ● | ● | ● | ● | ● | ● | ● | ● | ● | ● | ● | ● |
| 3.OA.4 | ● |  | ● |  | ● |  |  |  | ● | ● |  | ● | ● | ● | ● | ● |  | ● |  | ● |
| 3.OA.5 |  |  | ● |  |  |  | ● |  |  |  |  | ● |  | ● |  |  |  | ● |  | ● |
| 3.OA.6 | ● |  | ● | ● | ● | ● | ● |  | ● |  | ● |  | ● |  | ● | ● |  | ● | ● | ● |
| 3.OA.7 | ● | ● | ● | ● | ● |  | ● | ● | ● | ● | ● | ● |  |  |  |  |  |  |  |  |
| 3.OA.8 |  | ● | ● | ● | ● |  | ● | ● | ● |  | ● | ● | ● |  | ● |  | ● | ● | ● |  |
| 3.OA.9 |  |  | ● |  | ● |  |  |  | ● |  |  | ● |  | ● | ● | ● | ● | ● |  | ● |
| 3.NBT.1 |  | ● |  | ● | ● |  | ● | ● |  |  | ● |  |  | ● |  | ● |  | ● |  | ● |
| 3.NBT.2 |  | ● |  | ● |  | ● |  |  | ● | ● | ● | ● | ● | ● |  |  |  |  |  |  |
| 3.NBT.3 |  | ● |  | ● |  | ● |  | ● |  |  |  | ● | ● | ● |  |  |  | ● | ● |  |
| 3.NF.1 | ● | ● | ● | ● | ● | ● | ● | ● | ● | ● | ● |  | ● |  |  | ● |  | ● |  | ● |
| 3.NF.2a | ● | ● | ● |  |  | ● | ● | ● |  |  |  |  | ● |  | ● |  | ● |  | ● |  |
| 3.NF.2b | ● | ● | ● | ● | ● | ● | ● | ● | ● | ● |  |  | ● |  | ● |  | ● |  | ● |  |
| 3.NF.3a | ● | ● | ● | ● | ● | ● | ● | ● | ● | ● | ● |  | ● |  | ● | ● | ● |  | ● | ● |
| 3.NF.3b | ● | ● | ● | ● | ● | ● | ● | ● | ● | ● | ● |  | ● |  | ● | ● | ● |  | ● | ● |
| 3.NF.3c | ● | ● | ● | ● | ● | ● | ● | ● | ● | ● |  |  |  |  |  |  | ● |  |  |  |
| 3.NF.3d | ● | ● | ● | ● | ● | ● | ● | ● | ● | ● | ● |  | ● |  | ● |  | ● |  |  |  |
| 3.MD.1 | ● |  | ● |  |  | ● |  |  |  | ● | ● | ● |  | ● | ● | ● |  | ● | ● | ● |
| 3.MD.2 |  |  |  |  |  |  |  |  |  |  | ● | ● | ● | ● | ● | ● | ● | ● | ● | ● |
| 3.MD.3 |  |  |  | ● |  |  |  |  |  |  |  | ● |  | ● |  |  |  |  |  |  |
| 3.MD.4 | ● | ● | ● | ● | ● | ● | ● | ● | ● | ● |  |  |  | ● | ● |  | ● |  |  | ● |
| 3.MD.5a |  |  |  |  |  |  |  |  |  |  | ● | ● |  |  |  |  |  |  |  |  |
| 3.MD.5b |  |  |  |  |  |  |  |  |  |  | ● | ● | ● | ● |  |  |  | ● |  |  |
| 3.MD.6 |  |  |  |  |  |  |  |  |  |  | ● | ● |  |  |  |  |  |  |  |  |
| 3.MD.7a |  |  |  |  |  |  |  |  |  |  |  |  | ● | ● |  |  |  | ● |  |  |
| 3.MD.7b |  |  |  |  |  |  |  |  |  |  |  |  |  |  |  | ● | ● | ● |  |  |
| 3.MD.7c |  |  |  |  |  |  |  |  |  |  |  |  | ● | ● |  |  |  | ● |  |  |
| 3.MD.7d |  |  |  |  |  |  |  |  |  |  |  |  |  |  |  |  |  |  | ● | ● |
| 3.MD.8 |  |  |  |  |  |  |  |  |  |  | ● | ● | ● | ● | ● | ● | ● | ● | ● | ● |
| 3.G.1 |  |  |  |  |  |  |  |  |  |  |  |  |  |  |  |  | ● |  |  |  |
| 3.G.2 | ● | ● | ● | ● | ● | ● | ● | ● | ● | ● |  |  |  |  |  |  |  | ● |  |  |

W = Week

CD-104592 • © Carson-Dellosa

**Day 1**

$97 + 75 = 172$

$90 + 7 \mid 70 + 5$

$90 + 70 =$

$160 + 5 + 2 =$

$172$

On Monday, Sarah read 24 pages of her book. On Tuesday night, she read 41 pages, and Wednesday night, she read 32 pages. How many pages did Sarah read altogether?

_97 pages_

What time is shown on the clock?

_3:30_

$18 - 5 = 13$

**Day 2**

$98 + 33 = 131$

$31 + 2$

$98 + 2 = 100$

$100 + 31 = 1,3,1$

Round the following numbers to the nearest 10.

13 _100_

21 _20_

_30_

29 _30_

How many more students voted for baseball and hockey than football? _3_

Total Votes

$45 + 88 = 133$

**Day 3**

Mandy made 27 pizzas. She made 16 pepperoni pizzas, 4 cheese pizzas, and the rest were sausage. How many sausage pizzas did Mandy make?

_7_

Round the following numbers to the nearest 100.

324 _300_

558 _600_

256 _300_

Color all of the quadrilaterals.

Write the number in standard form.

$500 + 30 + 3$

_533_

**Day 4**

$71 + 13 = 84$

$70 + 1 \mid 10 + 3$

$3 + 1 = 4$

$70 + 10 = 80$

Look at the base ten blocks. Write the number shown.

_443_

Write the missing numbers to complete the pattern.

2, 4, 6, 8,

_10_, _12_,

_14_, _16_,

_18_, _20_,

Becca put 91 books on a shelf. Of the books, 28 were nonfiction, 13 were poetry books, and the rest were fiction books. How many books were fiction?

_50_

Name _Camille June_

1. Round the following numbers to the nearest 10.

   15 _20_

   28 _30_

   52 _50_

2. What time is shown on the clock?

   _8:00_

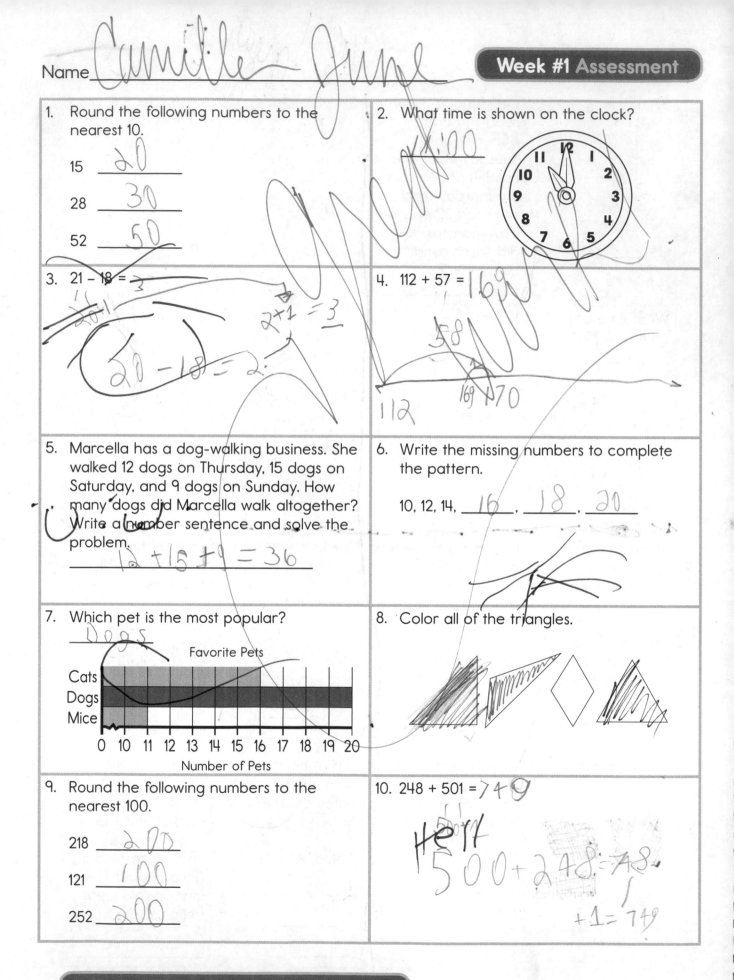

3. 21 – 18 = _3_

   2 + 1 = 3

   20 – 18 = 2

4. 112 + 57 = _169_

   58

   169  170

   112

5. Marcella has a dog-walking business. She walked 12 dogs on Thursday, 15 dogs on Saturday, and 9 dogs on Sunday. How many dogs did Marcella walk altogether? Write a number sentence and solve the problem.

   _12 + 15 + 9 = 36_

6. Write the missing numbers to complete the pattern.

   10, 12, 14, _16_, _18_, _20_

7. Which pet is the most popular?

   _Dogs_

   **Favorite Pets**

   Cats

   Dogs

   Mice

   0  10  11  12  13  14  15  16  17  18  19  20

   Number of Pets

8. Color all of the triangles.

9. Round the following numbers to the nearest 100.

   218 _200_

   121 _100_

   252 _200_

10. 248 + 501 = _749_

    Hell

    500 + 248 = 748

    +1 = 749

3.OA.9, 3.NBT.1, 3.NBT.2, 3.MD.1, 3.MD.3, 3.G.1     CD-104592 • © Carson-Dellosa

Name_____

**Day 1**

Round the following numbers to the nearest 100.

634 __600__

268 __300__

489 __500__

55 + 84 = *139*

*50 + 80 = 130*

*139*

*4 + 5 = 9*

What is the name of the figure shown?

__pentagon__

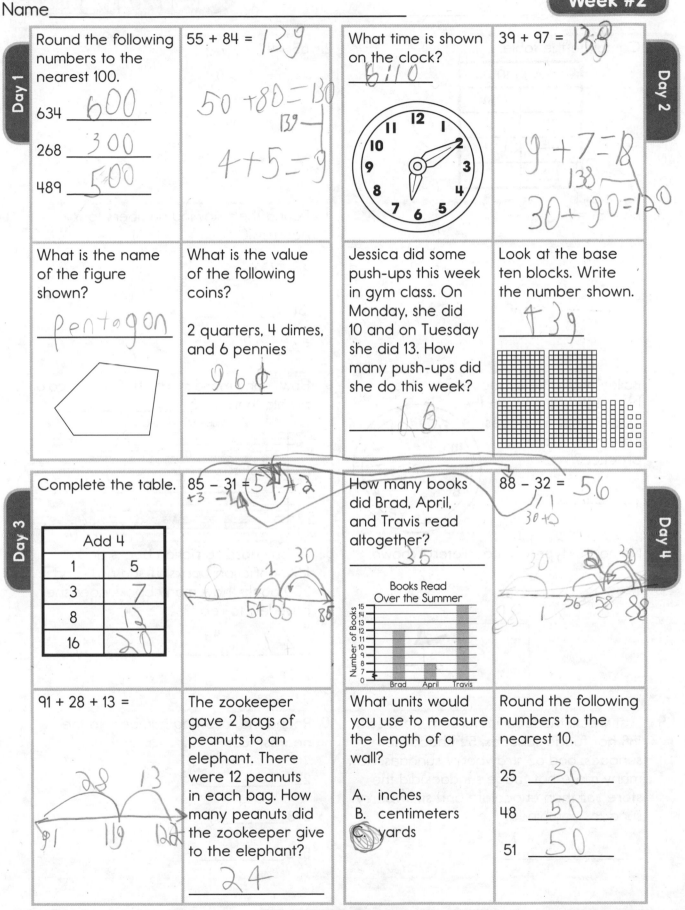

What is the value of the following coins?

2 quarters, 4 dimes, and 6 pennies

__96¢__

**Day 2**

What time is shown on the clock?

__6:10__

39 + 97 = *138*

*9 + 7 = 16*

*138*

*30 + 90 = 120*

Jessica did some push-ups this week in gym class. On Monday, she did 10 and on Tuesday she did 13. How many push-ups did she do this week?

__16__

Look at the base ten blocks. Write the number shown.

__439__

**Day 3**

Complete the table.

| Add 4 | |
|---|---|
| 1 | 5 |
| 3 | 7 |
| 8 | 12 |
| 16 | 20 |

85 – 31 = *54 + 2*

*+3 –1*

*5 + 55 = 85*

91 + 28 + 13 =

*28  13*

*91  119  122*

The zookeeper gave 2 bags of peanuts to an elephant. There were 12 peanuts in each bag. How many peanuts did the zookeeper give to the elephant?

__24__

**Day 4**

How many books did Brad, April, and Travis read altogether?

__35__

Books Read Over the Summer

88 – 32 = *56*

*30 + 0*

*56  58  88*

What units would you use to measure the length of a wall?

A. inches
B. centimeters
C. yards

Round the following numbers to the nearest 10.

25 __30__

48 __50__

51 __50__

Name_____

1. Complete the table.

| Add 10 | |
|---|---|
| 41 | 51 |
| 57 | 67 |
| 47 | 51 |
| 52 | 62 |

2. 65 + 47 = 112

$$60 + 40 = 100$$

$$100 + 7 + 5 = 112$$

3. 86 − 51 = 35

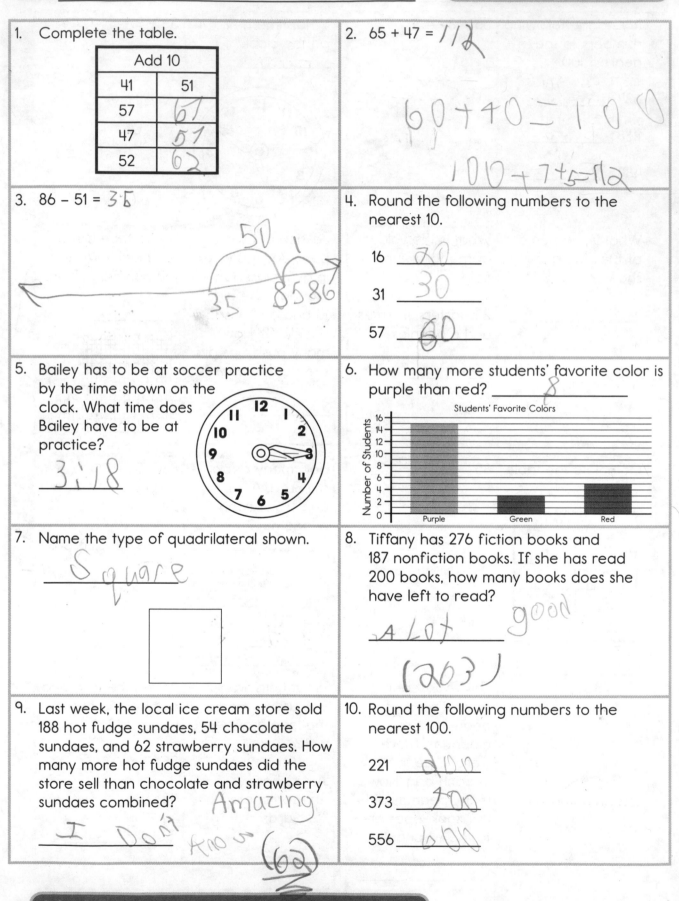

4. Round the following numbers to the nearest 10.

16 _____ 20

31 _____ 30

57 _____ 60

5. Bailey has to be at soccer practice by the time shown on the clock. What time does Bailey have to be at practice?

3:18

6. How many more students' favorite color is purple than red? _____ 8

Students' Favorite Colors

7. Name the type of quadrilateral shown.

Square

8. Tiffany has 276 fiction books and 187 nonfiction books. If she has read 200 books, how many books does she have left to read?

A Lot    good

(263)

9. Last week, the local ice cream store sold 188 hot fudge sundaes, 54 chocolate sundaes, and 62 strawberry sundaes. How many more hot fudge sundaes did the store sell than chocolate and strawberry sundaes combined?    Amazing

I Don't know    (62)

10. Round the following numbers to the nearest 100.

221 _____ 200

373 _____ 400

556 _____ 600

3.OA.8, 3.OA.9, 3.NBT.1, 3.NBT.2, 3.MD.1, 3.MD.3, 3.G.1    CD-104592 • © Carson-Dellosa

11

Name_____

**Day 1**

Jamie has to watch her little sister at the time shown on the clock. What time does Jamie have to watch her little sister?

8:15

748 − 459 = 281

700-400=
300 +
59 + 18 =
281

Write the following number in expanded form.

548

500, 40, 8

Complete the table.

| Subtract 11 | |
| --- | --- |
| 23 | 12 |
| 78 | 67 |
| 34 | 23 |

**Day 2**

How many students' birthdays are in January, February, and March? 11

Student Birthdays, by Month

4 + 8 = 12

3 + 2 = 5

8 + 3 = 11

Count by 5s.

405, 410, 415,

420,

425,

430

Round the following numbers to the nearest 10.

37  40

65  70

81  81

**Day 3**

What shape has 6 sides and 6 vertices?

hextagon

4 − 0 = 4

12 − 4 = 8

4 − 2 = 2

Owen is going to visit his aunt. He travels 278 miles on Saturday. He travels 81 miles farther on Sunday than he did on Saturday. How many miles did Owen travel on Sunday?

359

Round the following numbers to the nearest 100.

736  700

397  400

890  900

**Day 4**

Sally's twin brother, Sean, has 348 fiction books and 109 nonfiction books. If Sean has read 300 books, how many books has Sean not read?

157

Brooke has 7 dimes, 4 quarters, and 8 pennies in her pocket. How much money does Brooke have?

$1.78

Is this set of baseballs even or odd? yes

634 + 268 = 902

68 + 34 =
102

600 + 200 = 800 +
102 = 902

© Carson-Dellosa • CD-104592

13

Name _____Cari_____

1. Amy has to be at swim practice by the time shown on the clock. What time does Amy have to be at swim practice?

   **7:15**

2. Shannon's favorite book is *Traveling without Shoes*. The book has 214 pages of text and 122 pages of pictures. If Shannon is on page 325, how many more pages until she gets to the end of the book?

   **41** ✓

3. Round the following numbers to the nearest 100.

   455 **500**

   201 **200**

   616 **600** ✓

4. What is the name of a shape that has 3 sides and 1 right angle?

5. Which type of tree was planted the most this year? **Pine**

   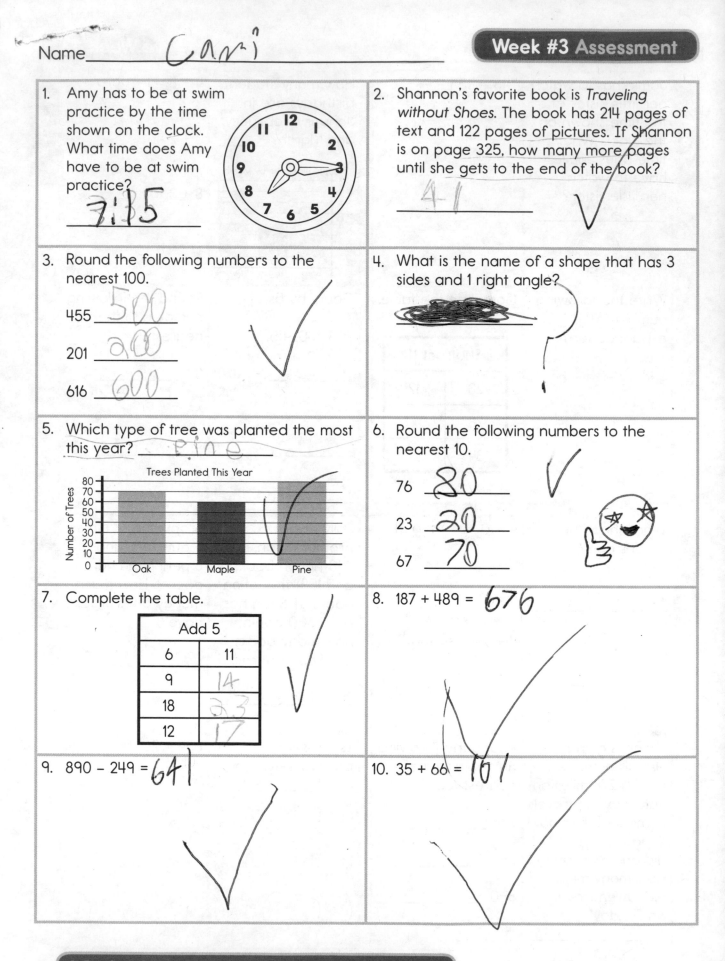

   Trees Planted This Year

   (bar graph: Number of Trees vs. Oak, Maple, Pine)

6. Round the following numbers to the nearest 10.

   76 **80** ✓

   23 **20**

   67 **70**

7. Complete the table. ✓

   | Add 5 | |
   |---|---|
   | 6 | 11 |
   | 9 | 14 |
   | 18 | 23 |
   | 12 | 17 |

8. 187 + 489 = **676** ✓

9. 890 – 249 = **641** ✓

10. 35 + 66 = **101** ✓

Name _____

**Day 1**

Delaney's favorite book is *Trees in the Breeze*. The book has 85 pages of text and 145 pages of pictures. If Delaney is on page 197, how many pages are left to read?

_____

15 + 15 =

What fraction does this circle show?

_____

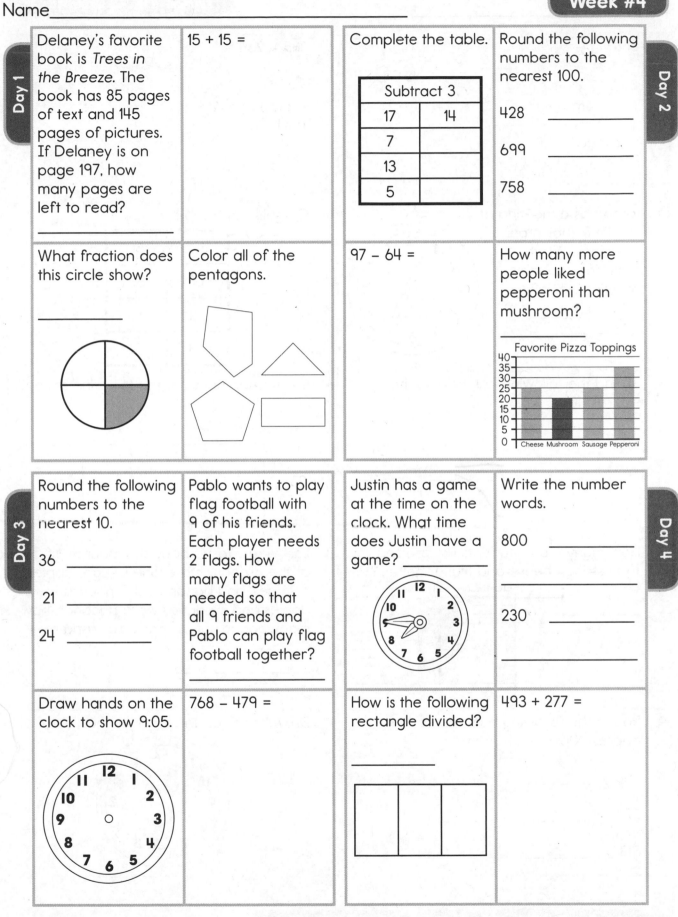

Color all of the pentagons.

**Day 2**

Complete the table.

| Subtract 3 | |
| --- | --- |
| 17 | 14 |
| 7 | |
| 13 | |
| 5 | |

Round the following numbers to the nearest 100.

428 _____

699 _____

758 _____

97 – 64 =

How many more people liked pepperoni than mushroom?

Favorite Pizza Toppings

(bar graph: Cheese 25, Mushroom 20, Sausage 25, Pepperoni 35; y-axis 0–40)

**Day 3**

Round the following numbers to the nearest 10.

36 _____

21 _____

24 _____

Pablo wants to play flag football with 9 of his friends. Each player needs 2 flags. How many flags are needed so that all 9 friends and Pablo can play flag football together?

_____

Draw hands on the clock to show 9:05.

768 – 479 =

**Day 4**

Justin has a game at the time on the clock. What time does Justin have a game? _____

Write the number words.

800 _____

_____

230 _____

_____

How is the following rectangle divided?

_____

493 + 277 =

© Carson-Dellosa • CD-104592

1. 888 + 77 =

2. 385 − 269 =

3. Reba has a meeting at the time shown on the clock. What time does Reba's meeting begin?

_____

4. Complete the table.

| Subtract 50 | |
| --- | --- |
| 103 | 53 |
| 121 | |
| 113 | |

5. Round the following numbers to the nearest 10.

35 _____

64 _____

14 _____

6. What is the name of the following shape?

_____

7. How many more students like pretzels than string cheese and fruit together?

_____

Favorite Snacks of Students

8. Last week, Tasha bought 17 pounds of fruit at the grocery store. She bought apples, oranges, and bananas. If 8 pounds were apples and 3 pounds were bananas, how many pounds of oranges did Tasha buy?

_____

9. Round the following numbers to the nearest 100.

296 _____

273 _____

319 _____

10. Draw hands on the clock to show 7:40.

3.OA.8, 3.OA.9, 3.NBT.1, 3.NBT.2, 3.MD.1, 3.MD.3, 3.G.1      CD-104592 • © Carson-Dellosa

**Day 1**

Complete the table.

| Add 34 | |
|---|---|
| 50 | 84 |
| 20 | |
| 0 | |
| 30 | |

Write the fraction that is represented by this rectangle.

_____

**Day 2**

How many sit-ups did Conner do on Monday, Tuesday, and Wednesday?

_____

Connor's Sit-Ups

If 3 students read 4 books each, how many books did the students read in all?

_____

Round each number to the nearest 10. Then, add.

41 + 129 is about

_____

In one hour, Miranda hiked 342 feet. In another two hours, Miranda hiked 512 feet. If the mountain is 1,000 feet high, how many more feet does Miranda have to hike? _____

Write the number in standard form.

600 + 20 + 4

_____

732 + 199 =

**Day 3**

What time is shown on the clock?

_____

How is the following circle divided?

_____

**Day 4**

Round each number to the nearest 100. Then, add.

277 + 338 is about

_____

Write the missing numbers to complete the pattern.

3, 6, 9, _____,

15, _____,

_____

A total of 219 students signed up to take swimming lessons. If 174 students are under 10 years old, how many students are over 10 years old?

_____

837 – 209 =

What is the value of the number 7 in the following number?

987

_____

What is the name of the quadrilateral that has 4 equal sides and 4 right angles?

_____

Name_____

1. What is the name of the quadrilateral shown?

   _____

2. Complete the table.

   | Add 49 | |
   |---|---|
   | 30 | 79 |
   | 42 | |
   | 37 | |
   | 45 | |

3. What time is shown on the clock?

   _____

4. 276 + 647 =

5. 837 – 209 =

6. Round each number to the nearest 100. Then, add.

   741 + 176 is about _____

7. Luke needs 415 balloons for a party. He has 166 and his mom gives him 120 more. How many more balloons does Luke need to get for the party?

   _____

8. 72 – 12 =

9. Round each number to the nearest 10. Then, add.

   187 + 68 is about _____

10. Write the missing numbers to complete the pattern.

    76, 82, 88, _____, _____, _____

Name_____

**Day 1**

What is the name of the quadrilateral with 2 pairs of equal sides and 2 pairs of opposite angles that are equal?

_____

$7 + 3 =$

$8 + 7 =$

$9 + 7 =$

**Day 2**

$394 + 496 =$

Write the number.

five hundred sixty-three

_____

---

Lola has 3 dollar bills, 6 quarters, and 4 dimes. How much money does Lola have?

_____

Patrick bought a bag of mixed nuts and raisins. If there are 342 peanuts, 176 cashews, and 256 raisins, how many total pieces are in the bag?

_____

Draw an array to match the equation.

$5 + 5 + 5 = 15$

How many students liked chocolate and vanilla?

_____

Favorite Ice Cream Flavors

---

**Day 3**

$476 - 267 =$

Write <, >, or = to make the statements true.

164 ◯ 146

578 ◯ 587

902 ◯ 902

**Day 4**

Penny has to go to bed at the time shown on the clock. What time does Penny have to go to bed?

_____

How many centimeters long is the paintbrush?

_____

---

Count by 100s.

594, 694, _____,

894, _____

Complete the number pattern.

66, 69, 72,

_____,

_____,

_____

Describe how this circle is divided.

_____

Round each number to the nearest 10. Then, add.

113 + 76 is about

_____

Name_____

1. Complete the number pattern.

   14, 21, 28, _____ , _____ , _____

2. 557 + 323 =

3. 689 − 478 =

4. Round each number to the nearest 10. Then, add.

   594 + 255 is about _____

5. How many people were surveyed for this bar graph? _____

   Favorite Fair Food

6. Olivia baked some cookies. Of the cookies, 124 were chocolate chip, 85 were peanut butter, and 91 were oatmeal. How many cookies did Olivia make?

   _____

7. Neil has to be at Parker's birthday party at the time shown on the clock. What time does Neil have to be at Parker's birthday party?

   _____

8. What is the name of a figure that has 6 equal-sized faces?

   _____

9. Round each number to the nearest 100. Then, add.

   486 + 313 is about _____

10. 56 + 35 =

    95 + 68 =

## Day 1

Wendy has to go to the movies at the time shown on the clock. What time does Wendy have to go to the movies? _____

$450 - 10 =$

$611 + 100 =$

$321 + 10 =$

Look at the base ten blocks. Write the number shown.

_____

$677 - 288 =$

## Day 2

Complete the table.

| Subtract 9 | |
|---|---|
| 15 | 6 |
| 24 | |
| 20 | |
| 12 | |

Is this set of objects even or odd? _____

$36 + 27 =$

$68 - 33 =$

How many more blue cars were in the parking lot than red cars?

_____

Colors of Cars

## Day 3

Round each number to the nearest 100. Then, add.

$264 + 456$ is about

_____

$272 + 301 =$

Delinda has 95 pencils. If 33 are blue, 41 are red, and 21 are green, how many pencils are red or green?

_____

Norman has 143 fish. He has goldfish, clown fish, and angelfish. If he has 73 goldfish and 29 clown fish, how many angelfish does Norman have?

_____

$254 + 347 =$

How many more students go to bed at 9:00 than at 8:00? _____

| Third Graders' Bedtimes | |
|---|---|
| 8:00 | ◇ ◇ |
| 8:30 | ◇ |
| 9:00 | ◇ ◇ ◇ ◇ |

◇ = 4 students

## Day 4

Round each number to the nearest 10. Then, add.

$82 + 33$ is about

_____

Write the name of the shape that has no sides and no vertices.

_____

1. For what favorite subjects did the same number of students vote? _____

Favorite Subjects

Number of Students
16
14
12
10
8
6
4
2
0
Reading    Math    Music    PE

2. Dawn's aquarium has 209 rocks, plants and pieces of seaweed in it. She has 187 rocks and 4 plants. How many pieces of seaweed does Dawn's aquarium have?

_____

3. Complete the table.

| Subtract 20 | |
|---|---|
| 160 | 140 |
| 140 | |
| 200 | |
| 180 | |

4. What time is shown on the clock?

_____

5. Round each number to the nearest 100. Then, add.

173 + 230 is about _____

6. 665 + 331 =

7. 376 – 187 =

8. Color all of the shapes that have 3 vertices.

9. Round each number to the nearest 10. Then, add.

57 + 63 is about _____

10. Ginny caught 73 shrimp. Hunter caught 15 fewer shrimp than Ginny. Trey caught 93 shrimp. How many shrimp did Ginny, Hunter, and Trey catch altogether?

_____

3.OA.8, 3.OA.9, 3.NBT.1, 3.NBT.2, 3.MD.1, 3.MD.3, 3.G.1    CD-104592 • © Carson-Dellosa

Name_____

**Day 1**

How many more trees were planted in September than November? _____

**Trees Planted**

| September | 🌲🌲🌲🌲 |
| October | 🌲🌲🌲🌲 |
| November | 🌲🌲 |

🌲 = 4 trees

There are 567 people who want tickets to a concert. There are only 417 tickets available. How many people will not be able to get tickets?

_____

About how many people entered the Bake-Off in 2001 and 2002? _____

Bake-Off Entries

$15 + 37 + 10 =$

**Day 2**

$493 + 229 =$

Round each number to the nearest 10. Then, add.

$196 + 715$ is about

_____

Write the number word.

212 _____

_____

Round each number to the nearest 100. Then, add.

$261 + 487$ is about

_____

**Day 3**

Write the missing numbers to complete the pattern.
145, 148, 151,

_____,

_____,

_____

Fill in the blanks with <, >, or = to make each number sentence true.

315 ◯ 415

116 ◯ 116

649 ◯ 694

Fiona takes her puppy to the park at the time shown on the clock. What time is shown on the clock?

_____

Melissa placed 4 pictures on each of the 5 shelves in her bedroom. How many pictures did Melissa place on the shelves in all?

_____

**Day 4**

$521 - 294 =$

Tyler drove 500 miles last week. On Monday, he drove 146 miles, and on Tuesday, he drove 200 miles. How many miles did Tyler drive the rest of the week?

_____

What does the number 8 stand for in the number 687?

_____

Color all of the shapes that have 4 vertices.

1. Color all of the shapes that have 4 sides.

2. Ashton bought 95 erasers. He gave 24 to his little sister and gave 65 to his teacher. How many erasers does Ashton have left?

   _____

3. 288 + 348 =

4. 387 − 329 =

5. What time is shown on the clock?

   _____

6. Write the missing numbers to complete the pattern.

   204, 208, 212, _____, _____, _____

7. Round each number to the nearest 10. Then, add.

   251 + 524 is about _____

8. Round each number to the nearest 100. Then, add.

   89 + 258 is about _____

9. About how many starfish and fish were observed? _____

   Sea Animals Observed

   Number of Animals

   Starfish   Clams   Dolphins   Fish

10. How many more students had dogs and cats than fish and birds? _____

    🐾 = 1 pet

    Students' Pets

    | Dogs | |
    | Cats | |
    | Fish | |
    | Birds | |

3.OA.8, 3.OA.9, 3.NBT.1, 3.NBT.2, 3.MD.1, 3.MD.3, 3.G.1

CD-104592 • © Carson-Dellosa

Name_____

**Day 1**

376 + 266 =

---

Round each number to the nearest 100. Then, add.

612 + 303 is about

_____

---

Write each number in standard form.

600 + 90 + 3

_____

500 + 40 + 2

_____

100 + 2

_____

---

How many letters were mailed on Monday, Tuesday, and Wednesday?

_____

| Letters Mailed | |
|---|---|
| Monday | ✉✉✉ |
| Tuesday | ✉✉ |
| Wednesday | ✉✉ |

✉ = 8 letters

**Day 2**

301 – 242 =

---

Circle the hexagon.

---

How many inches long is the fork?

_____

---

Fill in the missing numbers to complete the pattern.
175, 181, 187,

_____,

_____,

_____

**Day 3**

The movie theater has 500 seats. Ms. Avery's class takes 33 seats, and Ms. Hamilton's class takes 27 seats. How many seats are left for Mr. Daniel's class?

_____

---

444 + 279 =

---

Yolanda has $2.16. Ruby gives Yolanda 3 dimes and 4 pennies. How much money does Yolanda have now?

_____

---

Round each number to the nearest 10. Then, add.

491 + 203 is about

_____

**Day 4**

Mia has to meet Laura at the pool at 10:45. Draw hands on the clock to show that time.

---

12 – 4 =

11 – 9 =

3 + 7 =

---

Count by 100s.

578, 678,

_____,

_____,

_____

---

How many more people picked apple juice than grape juice?

_____

Most Popular Juice

Name_____

1. How many wins did the Angels and Cardinals have combined?

   _____

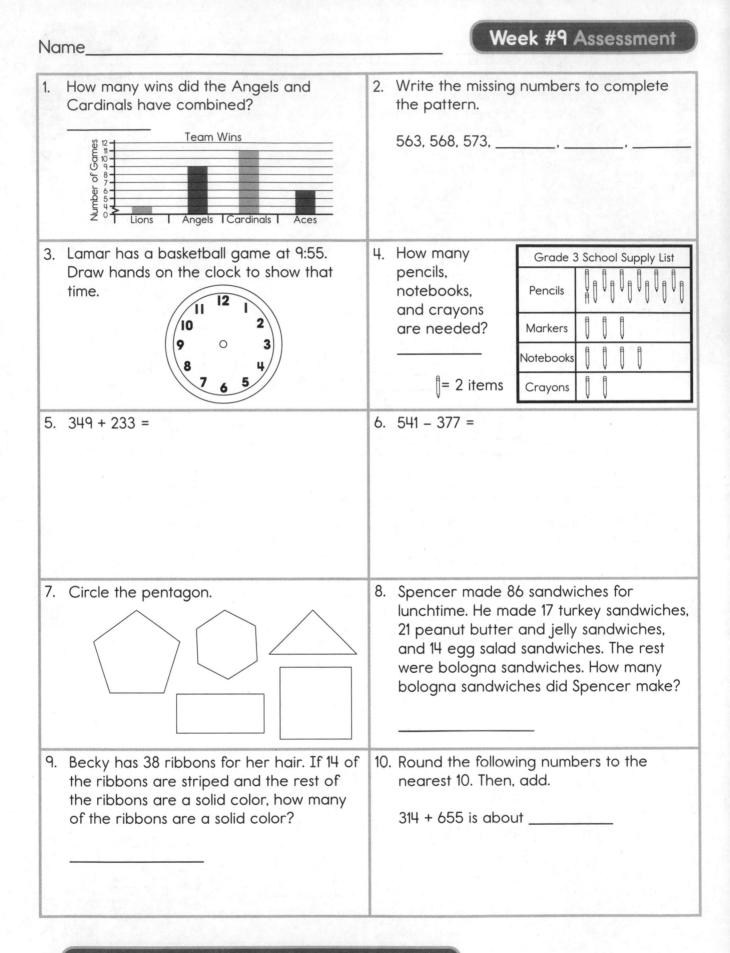

2. Write the missing numbers to complete the pattern.

   563, 568, 573, _____, _____, _____

3. Lamar has a basketball game at 9:55. Draw hands on the clock to show that time.

4. How many pencils, notebooks, and crayons are needed?

   _____

   ▯ = 2 items

   | Grade 3 School Supply List | |
   | --- | --- |
   | Pencils | |
   | Markers | |
   | Notebooks | |
   | Crayons | |

5. 349 + 233 =

6. 541 – 377 =

7. Circle the pentagon.

8. Spencer made 86 sandwiches for lunchtime. He made 17 turkey sandwiches, 21 peanut butter and jelly sandwiches, and 14 egg salad sandwiches. The rest were bologna sandwiches. How many bologna sandwiches did Spencer make?

   _____

9. Becky has 38 ribbons for her hair. If 14 of the ribbons are striped and the rest of the ribbons are a solid color, how many of the ribbons are a solid color?

   _____

10. Round the following numbers to the nearest 10. Then, add.

    314 + 655 is about _____

26  3.OA.8, 3.OA.9, 3.NBT.1, 3.NBT.2, 3.MD.1, 3.MD.3, 3.G.1

Name_____

**Day 1**

Round each number to the nearest 100. Then, add.

725 + 241 is about

_____

---

Last year, school was held 180 days. Mason was absent 9 days during the year. How many days did Mason attend school?

_____

---

Jonathan should have 156 items. He has 45 sandwiches, 24 cookies, and 40 bottles of water. How many items did Jonathan forget?

_____

---

**Day 2**

Write each number.
six hundred seventy-two

_____

two hundred fifty-one

_____

---

Draw hands on the clock to show 6:19.

---

249 + 307 =

---

Write the missing numbers to complete the pattern.
65, 74, 83,

_____ ,

_____ ,

_____

---

133 + 76 =

---

**Day 3**

How many more cars were parked on Wednesday than on Tuesday?

_____

Cars Parked on Ave. D

| Mon. | 🚗🚗 |
| Tues. | 🚗🚗🚗 |
| Wed. | 🚗🚗🚗🚗🚗 |

🚗 = 6 cars

---

Add or subtract mentally.

651 + 100 = _____

495 – 10 = _____

---

How much more did the Parks' electric bill cost in July than in May? _____

The Parks' Electric Bill

---

**Day 4**

Nellie has $3.42. She gives Vanessa 4 quarters. How much money does Nellie have left?

_____

---

Round each number to the nearest 10. Then, add.

615 + 348 is about

_____

---

417 – 78 =

---

Draw two different shapes that each have 5 sides.

---

26 + 17 =

---

1. Draw hands on the clock to show 10:59.

2. 271 – 198 =

3. Laura spun a red, blue, and green spinner 100 times. It landed on red 23 times and blue 51 times. How many times did it land on green?

_____

4. Round each number to the nearest 100. Then, add.

457 + 312 is about _____

5. Write the missing numbers to complete the pattern.

425, 400, _____, 350, 325, _____

6. Where did the most students spend their vacations? _____

| Summer Vacation Places | |
| --- | --- |
| Beach | 👣👣 |
| Mountains | 👣👣👣 |
| Home | 👣 |

👣 = 5 students

7. 505 + 404 =

8. Draw two different shapes that each have at least 3 vertices.

9. Round the following numbers to the nearest 10. Then, add.

84 + 328 is about _____

10. How many more newspapers did Lee deliver during week 2 than during week 3? _____

Newspapers Lee Delivered in June

Week 3
Week 2
Week 1

0  65  70  75  80  85  90  95  100  105  110  115
Number of Newspapers Delivered

3.OA.8, 3.OA.9, 3.NBT.1, 3.NBT.2, 3.MD.1, 3.MD.3, 3.G.1     CD-104592 • © Carson-Dellosa

Name_____

**Day 1**

If 4 students read 4 books each, how many books did the students read in all? Write an equation and solve the problem.

_____

What time is shown on the clock?

_____

A swimming pool has 20 swimmers. An equal number of swimmers are in the deep end and in the shallow end of the pool. How many swimmers are in each end of the pool?

_____

**Day 2**

37 + 222 =

---

211 + 418 =

2 × 0 = _____

2 × 8 = _____

6 × 2 = _____

Round each number to the nearest 10. Then, add.

166 + 341 is about

_____

10 × 1 = _____

10 × 2 = _____

10 × 3 = _____

---

**Day 3**

9 × _____ = 9

_____ × 2 = 2

7 × 0 = _____

Each of 8 girls has a button collection. Each girl has 8 buttons in her collection. How many total buttons are there in the 8 collections?

_____

Which equation is the same as 3 × 2 – 6?

A.  2 × 3 = 6
B.  6 × 3 = 18
C.  3 × 6 = 18
D.  6 × 2 = 12

**Day 4**

301 – 89 =

---

149 – 121 =

Write the missing numbers to complete the pattern.
12, 18, 24,

_____,

_____,

_____

Circle the rectangle.

1 × 8 = _____

5 × 2 = _____

9 × 2 = _____

Name_____

1. $4 \times 2 =$ _____

   $5 \times 1 =$ _____

   $2 \times 1 =$ _____

2. The PE teacher had 6 balls to give to 6 teams. How many balls did the teacher give to each team?

   _____

3. $6 \times$ _____ $= 0$

   _____ $\times 1 = 6$

   $2 \times 8 =$ _____

4. Which equation is the same as $8 \times 0 = 0$?

   A. $0 \times 0 = 0$
   B. $8 \times 3 = 24$
   C. $0 \times 8 = 0$
   D. $3 \times 8 = 24$

5. $10 \times 4 =$ _____

   $10 \times 5 =$ _____

   $10 \times 6 =$ _____

6. Write the missing numbers to complete the pattern.

   14, 17, 20, _____, _____, _____

7. There are 7 days in a week. There are about 4 weeks in a month. About how many days are in a month?

   _____

8. $678 + 287 =$

9. $471 - 382 =$

10. $7 \times$ _____ $= 14$

    $3 \times$ _____ $= 0$

    _____ $\times 2 = 8$

3.OA.3, 3.OA.4, 3.OA.5, 3.OA.7, 3.OA.9, 3.NBT.2, 3.NBT.3    CD-104592 • © Carson-Dellosa

Name_____

**Day 1**

$1 \times 0 =$ _____

$4 \times 0 =$ _____

$2 \times 2 =$ _____

---

$500 - 250 =$

---

**Day 2**

There are 8 bicycles available for rent at the bike shop. Each bike has 2 wheels. How many wheels in all are on the bikes that are available to rent? Write an equation and solve the problem.

_____

---

Round each number to the nearest 100. Then, add.

$112 + 208$ is about

_____

---

Joey is running a 26-mile marathon. Joey takes a break after 4 miles. He then runs 8 miles more before taking a second break. How many miles does Joey have left to run?

_____

---

Write the missing numbers to complete the pattern.
56, 54, 52,

_____ ,

_____ ,

---

What time is shown on the clock?

_____

---

$10 \times 7 =$ _____

$10 \times 8 =$ _____

$10 \times 9 =$ _____

---

**Day 3**

How many people visited a park in 2010 and 2011?

_____

Visitors to a Park

---

$4 \times$ _____ $= 4$

$5 \times$ _____ $= 0$

_____ $\times 7 = 7$

---

**Day 4**

Which equation is the same as $2 \times 9 = 18$?

A. $6 \times 3 = 18$
B. $9 \times 2 = 18$
C. $3 \times 6 = 18$
D. $5 \times 2 = 10$

---

$301 + 67 =$

---

$3 \times 7 = 21$

Write a related multiplication sentence.

_____

---

There are 9 rows of 9 computers. How many computers are in the office altogether?

_____

---

$3 \times$ _____ $= 9$

$3 \times$ _____ $= 0$

_____ $\times 1 = 2$

---

$2 \times 6 =$ _____

$1 \times 9 =$ _____

$1 \times 1 =$ _____

1. A zoo has 7 habitats with 2 monkeys in each habitat. How many total monkeys are in the 7 habitats?

   _____

2. $3 \times$ _____ $= 6$

   _____ $\times 3 = 24$

   $3 \times 7 =$ _____

3. $3 \times 4 = 12$

   Write a related multiplication sentence.

   _____

4. $3 \times 8 =$ _____

   $4 \times 3 =$ _____

   $2 \times 2 =$ _____

5. $10 \times 2 =$ _____

   $10 \times 5 =$ _____

   $10 \times 8 =$ _____

6. Write the missing numbers to complete the pattern.

   65, 62, 59, _____, _____, _____

7. $10 \times$ _____ $= 30$

   _____ $\times 6 = 12$

   $2 \times$ _____ $= 0$

8. Jasper visited the reptile house at the zoo and saw 45 lizards, snakes and turtles. If he saw 12 lizards and 26 snakes, how many turtles did Jasper see at the reptile house?

   _____

9. $318 + 71 =$

10. A group of 8 children are taking piano lessons. They each practice piano 2 hours a day. How many hours in all do the children practice?

    _____

 3.OA.3, 3.OA.4, 3.OA.5, 3.OA.7, 3.OA.8, 3.OA.9, 3.NBT.2, 3.NBT.3   CD-104592 • © Carson-Dellosa

Name_____

**Day 1**

$3 \times 5 = 15$

Write a related multiplication sentence.

_____

$2 \times 9 =$ _____

$9 \times 2 =$ _____

$8 \times 2 =$ _____

Ross is reading a book that has 584 pages. He read 171 pages on Saturday and 207 pages on Sunday. He finished the book on Monday. How many pages did he read on Monday?

$20 \times 2 =$ _____

$20 \times 3 =$ _____

$20 \times 4 =$ _____

**Day 2**

$5 \times$ _____ $= 10$

_____ $\times 7 = 14$

$9 \times 3 =$ _____

Harry has to be at work by the time shown on the clock. What time does Harry have to be at work?

_____

Kayla bought 5 boxes of Gingersnap Delights. Each box has 7 cookies. How many Gingersnap Delights does she have?

_____

$44 + 15 =$ _____

$82 - 30 =$ _____

**Day 3**

Jermaine bought 4 boxes of popcorn. Each box has 8 bags of popcorn. How many bags of popcorn does he have?

_____

$2 \times 4 =$ _____

$2 \times 3 =$ _____

$7 \times 3 =$ _____

Round each number to the nearest 10.

$34 + 81$ is about

_____

Write the multiplication sentence shown by the picture.

_____

**Day 4**

Complete the table.

| Multiply by 2 | |
|---|---|
| 2 | 4 |
| 3 | |
| 4 | |
| 5 | |
| 6 | |

$584 + 381 =$

$20 \times 5 =$ _____

$20 \times 6 =$ _____

$20 \times 7 =$ _____

$3 \times 6 =$ _____

$3 \times 3 =$ _____

$2 \times 8 =$ _____

1. Complete the table.

| Multiply by 2 | |
|---|---|
| 6 | 12 |
| 7 | |
| 8 | |
| 9 | |

2. $20 \times 6 =$ _____

   $20 \times 3 =$ _____

   $20 \times 8 =$ _____

3. Owen bought 3 boxes of Apple Puffs. Each box has 5 puffs. How many Apple Puffs does he have?

   _____

4. Write the multiplication sentence shown by the picture. _____

5. $2 \times$ _____ $= 18$

   _____ $\times 6 = 6$

   $3 \times 3 =$ _____

6. $4 \times 3 = 12$

   Write a related multiplication sentence.

   _____

7. $3 \times 2 =$ _____

   $2 \times 8 =$ _____

   $4 \times 1 =$ _____

8. Isabelle bought 7 boxes of Mixed Mints. Each box has 6 cookies. How many Mixed Mint cookies does she have?

   _____

9. $2 \times 5 = 10$

   Write a related multiplication sentence.

   _____

10. Yuri took pictures of 73 animals at the zoo. He took 14 pictures of monkeys, 21 pictures of the tigers, and 13 pictures of polar bears. How many pictures of other animals did Yuri take?

    _____

 3.OA.1, 3.OA.3, 3.OA.4, 3.OA.5, 3.OA.7, 3.OA.8, 3.OA.9, 3.NBT.3    CD-104592 • © Carson-Dellosa

Name_____

**Day 1**

30 × 2 = _____

30 × 3 = _____

30 × 4 = _____

---

Round each number to the nearest 10. Then, add.

678 + 179 is about

_____

---

Complete the table.

| Multiply by 3 | |
|---|---|
| 3 | 9 |
| 4 | |
| 5 | |
| 6 | |

---

504 + 298 =

**Day 2**

---

5 × 0 = _____

1 × 4 = _____

6 × 7 = _____

---

Ingrid is watching 2 spiders crawling on the sidewalk. The fuzzy spider crawls 3 times as far as the brown spider. The brown spider crawls 4 feet. How many feet does the fuzzy spider crawl?

_____

---

What was the weather mostly like last week?

_____

Weather Last Week

---

Which addition sentence is the same as 6 × 3?

A.  6 + 6

B.  3 + 3 + 3 + 3 + 3 + 3

C.  6 + 6 + 6

D.  3 + 3 + 3

---

**Day 3**

5 × 3 = 15

Write a related multiplication sentence.

_____

---

424 + 302 =

---

4 × _____ = 32

_____ × 9 = 36

2 × 4 = _____

---

What time is shown on the clock?

_____

**Day 4**

---

Anna mailed 10 invitations for her birthday party. She placed 4 stickers on the back of each invitation. How many stickers did she place on the invitations in all?

_____

---

5 × 4 = _____

3 × 8 = _____

9 × 2 = _____

---

168 – 134 =

---

Monica earned $20 doing chores. She went to the movies and bought a ticket for $9 and popcorn for $7. How much money does Monica have left?

_____

Name_____

1. $20 \times 7 =$ _____

   $10 \times 4 =$ _____

   $30 \times 3 =$ _____

2. Rusty earns $3 for each room he cleans in his house. Rusty cleans 2 rooms and buys a bag of candy for $2. How much money does he have left?

   _____

3. Complete the table.

   | Multiply by 3 | |
   |---|---|
   | 6 | 18 |
   | 7 | |
   | 8 | |
   | 9 | |

4. $2 \times$ _____ $= 10$

   _____ $\times 5 = 25$

   $4 \times 2 =$ _____

5. Henry is traveling by car to visit his grandmother. He listens to 3 of his favorite CDs before he arrives at his grandmother's house. Each CD has 6 songs. How many songs does Henry listen to while he is traveling?

   _____

6. Which multiplication fact matches the addition sentence?
   $8 + 8 + 8 + 8$

   A.  $2 \times 4$
   B.  $3 \times 8$
   C.  $4 \times 8$
   D.  $8 \times 3$

7. $8 \times 2 =$ _____

   $2 \times 1 =$ _____

   $8 \times 5 =$ _____

8. $3 \times 7 = 21$

   Write a related multiplication sentence.

   _____

9. Round each number to the nearest 10. Then, subtract.

   $701 - 299$ is about _____

10. A family of 5 is spending two weeks at the beach for vacation. Each family member is taking 2 swimsuits. How many swimsuits is the family taking?

    _____

Name_____

**Day 1**

Write the matching multiplication fact.

$5 + 5 + 5 + 5 + 5$

_____

$456 - 279 =$

**Day 2**

The mail carrier delivered letters to 8 houses on a city block. He delivered 3 letters to each house. How many letters did the mail carrier deliver?

_____

Write the multiplication sentence shown by the picture.

_____

Draw hands on the clock to show 7:26.

Complete the table.

| Multiply by 4 | |
|---|---|
| 1 | 4 |
| 2 | |
| 3 | |
| 4 | |
| 5 | |

Round each number to the nearest 10. Then, subtract.

$268 - 53$ is about

_____

$40 \times 2 =$ _____

$30 \times 6 =$ _____

$40 \times 3 =$ _____

**Day 3**

_____ $\times 5 = 35$

$8 \times$ _____ $= 32$

$3 \times 9 =$ _____

Color the quadrilateral.

$6 \times 7 = 42$

Write a related multiplication sentence.

_____

**Day 4**

Round each number to the nearest 100. Then, add.

$515 + 250$ is about

_____

Quinn earns $5 every hour she babysits. Quinn babysits for 6 hours. Then, she goes out for dinner and spends $14. How much money does she have left?

_____

$4 \times 4 =$ _____

$1 \times 9 =$ _____

$6 \times 3 =$ _____

$388 + 499 =$

Naomi has 45 red beads and 69 purple beads. She loses 16 beads while making a necklace. How many beads does Naomi have left?

_____

1. The Girls Club meets 3 times every week at their clubhouse. How many times do they meet in a 6-week period?

_____

2. Write the matching multiplication fact.

    $7 + 7 + 7$

    _____

3. _____ $\times 3 = 18$

    $1 \times$ _____ $= 8$

    $9 \times 6 =$ _____

4. $7 \times 8 = 56$

    Write the related multiplication fact.

    _____

5. $30 \times 7 =$ _____

    $40 \times 4 =$ _____

    $40 \times 5 =$ _____

6. Complete the table.

    | Multiply by 4 | |
    | --- | --- |
    | 5 | 20 |
    | 6 | |
    | 7 | |
    | 8 | |
    | 9 | |

7. Jackie has 19 dresses and 15 pairs of pants in her closet. If 9 pieces of her clothing are blue, how many pieces of Jackie's clothing are not blue?

    _____

8. $5 \times 2 =$ _____

    $7 \times 7 =$ _____

    $9 \times 3 =$ _____

9. $2 \times$ _____ $= 18$

    _____ $\times 7 = 56$

    _____ $\times 7 = 49$

10. Write the multiplication sentence shown by the picture.

    _____

 CD-104592 • © Carson-Dellosa

Name_____

**Day 1**

Draw 16 stars. Put them equally into 2 sets. How many stars are in each set?

_____

30 × 8 = _____

40 × 6 = _____

30 × 9 = _____

12 ÷ _____ = 3

_____ ÷ 5 = 3

21 ÷ 3 = _____

Terrance tackled a total of 42 football players in the last 6 games. He tackled the same number of players each game. How many players did Terrance tackle each game?

_____

---

Round each number to the nearest 10. Then, subtract.

497 − 315 is about

_____

10 ÷ 2 = _____

24 ÷ 3 = _____

9 ÷ 1 = _____

What time is shown on the clock?

_____

4 × 7 = _____

9 × 7 = _____

5 × 8 = _____

---

**Day 2**

Noah has 5 pieces of bubble gum to share with his 5 teammates. He wants to give each teammate the same number of pieces. How many pieces can Noah give each teammate?

_____

Abel drew some triangles. His drawing had 21 vertices. How many triangles did he draw? Write a division equation to answer the question.

_____

30 ÷ 6 = 5

Write a related multiplication sentence.

_____

40 ÷ 8 = _____

63 ÷ 7 = _____

45 ÷ 9 = _____

---

625 − 210 =

Complete the table.

| Multiply by 5 | |
|---|---|
| 2 | 10 |
| 3 | |
| 4 | |
| 5 | |
| 6 | |

50 × 2 = _____

60 × 2 = _____

60 × 3 = _____

If you add 5 to me and then divide by 9, you get 3. What number am I?

_____

**Day 3**  **Day 4**

Name_____

1. $9 \div$ _____ $= 3$

   _____ $\div 2 = 4$

   $14 \div 7 =$ _____

2. $21 \div 7 = 3$.

   Write a related multiplication sentence.

   _____

3. $16 \div 4 =$ _____

   $20 \div 5 =$ _____

   $18 \div 6 =$ _____

4. During their football season, the Kickerton Kangaroos had a combined total of 16 fumbles. Each of the 8 players had the same number of fumbles. How many fumbles did each player have?

   _____

5. Put 21 boxes into sets of 3. How many sets did you make? _____

6. Complete the table.

| Multiply by 5 | |
|---|---|
| 6 | 30 |
| 7 | |
| 8 | |
| 9 | |

7. $30 \times 3 =$ _____

   $40 \times 2 =$ _____

   $40 \times 5 =$ _____

8. If you multiply me by 7, subtract 2 and then divide by 6, you get 9. What number am I?

   _____

9. Twelve fans are going to the football game. There are 4 cars to take the fans to the game. The same number of fans will ride in each car. How many fans will ride in each car?

   _____

10. $8 \times 8 =$ _____

    $7 \times 5 =$ _____

    $1 \times 6 =$ _____

 3.OA.2, 3.OA.3, 3.OA.4, 3.OA.5, 3.OA.6, 3.OA.7, 3.OA.9, 3.NBT.3   CD-104592 • © Carson-Dellosa

**Day 1**

$50 \times 3 =$ _____

$60 \times 4 =$ _____

$50 \times 4 =$ _____

There are 8 girls in Katie's Girl Scout troop. Each girl decorated 3 gingerbread men. How many gingerbread men did the girls decorate altogether?

_____

$436 + 296 =$

$48 \div$ _____ $= 8$

_____ $\div 8 = 7$

$63 \div 9 =$ _____

**Day 2**

Complete the table.

| Multiply by 6 | |
|---|---|
| 2 | 12 |
| 3 | |
| 4 | |
| 5 | |
| 6 | |

$1 \times 2 =$ _____

$6 \times 2 =$ _____

$9 \times 5 =$ _____

$727 - 419 =$

Alexa knocked down 70 bowling pins in 10 frames. In each frame, Alexa knocked down the same number of pins. How many pins did Alexa knock down in each frame?

_____

**Day 3**

$28 \div 4 = 7$

Write a related multiplication sentence.

_____

Bonnie had 6 bags of 6 gel pens. She wanted to give the same number of gel pens to 9 friends. How many gel pens did each friend get?

_____

Round each number to the nearest 100. Then, subtract.

$187 - 69$ is about

_____

Draw 10 circles. Put them equally in 5 sets. How many circles are in each set?

_____

**Day 4**

Show two ways to solve this problem.

$4 \times 3 \times 2$

_____ $\div 8 = 2$

$27 \div$ _____ $= 3$

$32 \div 4 =$ _____

What time is shown on the clock?

_____

$36 \div 6 =$ _____

$16 \div 2 =$ _____

$40 \div 5 =$ _____

1. $50 \times 5 =$ _____

 $60 \times 5 =$ _____

 $50 \times 3 =$ _____

2. Complete the table.

| Multiply by 6 | |
|---|---|
| 6 | 36 |
| 7 | |
| 8 | |
| 9 | |

3. $54 \div 9 = 6$

 Write a related multiplication sentence.

 _____

4. Show two ways to solve this problem.

 $4 \times 5 \times 2$

5. _____ $\div 1 = 8$

 $27 \div$ _____ $= 9$

 $49 \div 7 =$ _____

6. Veronica will spend $30 to go bowling. Each game of bowling costs $6. How many games will Veronica bowl?

 _____

7. Put 12 hearts into sets of 4. How many sets did you make?

 _____

8. $9 \div 3 =$ _____

 $28 \div 7 =$ _____

 $64 \div 8 =$ _____

9. Jimmy had 8 boxes with 3 cars in each box. If Jimmy wanted to give each of his 4 friends an equal number of cars, how many cars would each friend get?

 _____

10. $1 \times 7 =$ _____

 $2 \times 6 =$ _____

 $6 \times 5 =$ _____

3.OA.2, 3.OA.3, 3.OA.4, 3.OA.5, 3.OA.7, 3.OA.8, 3.OA.9, 3.NBT.3

CD-104592 • © Carson-Dellosa

**Day 1**

$45 \div 5 = 9$

Write a related multiplication sentence.

_____

$3 + 3 + 3 + 3 + 3 + 3$

Write the matching multiplication fact.

_____

**Day 2**

Show two ways to solve this problem.

$3 \times 5 \times 2$

Round each number to the nearest 10. Then, subtract.

$765 - 323$ is about

_____

What time is shown on the clock?

_____

Put 7 moons into sets of 1. How many sets did you make?

_____

$7 \times 2 =$ _____

$6 \times 8 =$ _____

$8 \times 4 =$ _____

Jeremy uses 4 towels each time he washes his dad's car. He has washed his dad's car 2 times this month. How many towels did he use in all?

_____

**Day 3**

_____ $\div 5 = 7$

$24 \div$ _____ $= 4$

$28 \div 7 =$ _____

$348 + 248 =$

**Day 4**

Hugo lifted a total of 72 pounds in 9 attempts. Hugo lifted the same number of pounds in each attempt. How many pounds did he lift in each attempt?

_____

$848 - 399 =$

Heather baked 6 cupcakes each day for 2 days. She wanted to share her cupcakes with 4 friends. How many cupcakes did each friend get?

_____

$60 \times 6 =$ _____

$50 \times 5 =$ _____

$60 \times 7 =$ _____

$54 \div 6 =$ _____

$45 \div 5 =$ _____

$24 \div 4 =$ _____

Complete the table.

| Multiply by 7 | |
| --- | --- |
| 1 | 7 |
| 2 | |
| 3 | |
| 4 | |
| 5 | |

1. $16 \div 2 = 8$

   Write a related multiplication sentence.

   _____

2. Show two ways to solve this problem.

   $6 \times 2 \times 4$

3. _____ $\div 9 = 4$

   $72 \div$ _____ $= 9$

   $16 \div 2 =$ _____

4. Nine children lifted a combined total of 81 pounds. Each child lifted the same number of pounds. How many pounds did each child lift?

   _____

5. Draw 15 triangles. Put them equally into sets of 3. How many triangles are in each set?

   _____

6. $60 \times 8 =$ _____

   $50 \times 6 =$ _____

   $50 \times 7 =$ _____

7. Complete the table.

   | Multiply by 7 | |
   | --- | --- |
   | 5 | 35 |
   | 6 | |
   | 7 | |
   | 8 | |
   | 9 | |

8. $4 \div 1 =$ _____

   $42 \div 7 =$ _____

   $15 \div 3 =$ _____

9. Miguel earned 5 stickers each day for 4 days. On the fifth day he earned 2 stickers. How many stickers did Miguel earn in 5 days?

   _____

10. Solve this problem by writing the related multiplication fact.

    $15 \div 5 =$ _____ because

    _____ $\times$ _____ $= 15$

Name_____

**Day 1**

Round each number to the nearest 100. Then, subtract.

704 – 597 is about

_____

9 × 4 = _____

8 × 6 = _____

2 × 5 = _____

**Day 2**

Write the time shown on the clock.

_____

The pet store has 12 turtles. Nina feeds 2 lettuce leaves to each turtle. How many lettuce leaves does Nina feed the turtles?

_____

During the game, 36 players are sitting on 6 benches. The same number of players are sitting on each bench. How many players are sitting on each bench?

_____

36 ÷ 9 = 4

Write a related multiplication sentence.

_____

Holly has 56 pieces of paper and 8 paper clips. If she clips the same amount of paper together with each paper clip, how many pieces will be clipped together with each clip?

_____

Complete the table.

| Multiply by 8 | |
| --- | --- |
| 1 | 8 |
| 2 | |
| 3 | |
| 4 | |
| 5 | |

**Day 3**

How many total points were scored in the game?

_____

Points Scored in a Game

Nadia has 4 packs of gum that have 4 pieces each. If she wants to share her gum with 8 of her friends, how many pieces will each friend get?

_____

**Day 4**

Samantha is planting tomatoes. She plants 5 rows of 4 tomato seedlings. How many tomato seedlings does Samantha plant altogether?

_____

Lake Erie is 241 miles long. Lake Ontario is 193 miles long. How many miles long are Lake Erie and Lake Ontario altogether?

_____

54 ÷ _____ = 6

_____ ÷ 4 = 6

18 ÷ 3 = _____

40 × 7 = _____

30 × 8 = _____

50 × 8 = _____

Show two ways to solve this problem.

8 × 2 × 5

24 ÷ 8 = _____

30 ÷ 6 = _____

18 ÷ 2 = _____

© Carson-Dellosa • CD-104592

Name_____

1. Wyatt has a 40-ounce jug of water. Wyatt wants to give each of 5 basketball players the same amount of water. How many ounces of water can Walter give each player?

   _____

2. _____ ÷ 5 = 9

   12 ÷ _____ = 2

   32 ÷ 8 = _____

3. Show two ways to solve this problem.

   3 × 7 × 4

4. Dr. Underwood has 36 ribbons to give to 3 teachers in her school. If she gives the same number of ribbons to each teacher, how many ribbons will each teacher get?

   _____

5. Complete the table.

   | Multiply by 8 | |
   | --- | --- |
   | 5 | 40 |
   | 6 | |
   | 7 | |
   | 8 | |
   | 9 | |

6. 56 ÷ 8 = 7

   Write a related multiplication sentence.

   _____

7. 20 × 5 = _____

   30 × 9 = _____

   40 × 6 = _____

8. 48 ÷ 8 = _____

   27 ÷ 3 = _____

   4 ÷ 2 = _____

9. Perry earns $6 a day for 3 days. He wants to buy some toy models that cost $9 each. How many models can Perry buy with the money he has earned?

   _____

10. Leo is ordering more canary seed for the pet store. If the canaries eat 4 bags of seed in a month, how many bags will Leo need to order for the next 12 months?

    _____

3.OA.2, 3.OA.3, 3.OA.4, 3.OA.5, 3.OA.6, 3.OA.7, 3.OA.8, 3.OA.9, 3.NBT.3  CD-104592 • © Carson-Dellosa

**Day 1**

$7 \times 1 = $ _____

$2 \times 7 = $ _____

$3 \times 9 = $ _____

Lucy has 18 pansies, 12 geraniums, and 6 marigolds. If she divides the flowers equally between 3 flowerpots, how many flowers will each pot have?

_____

**Day 2**

$498 + 439 = $

Zane has 7 watering cans. Each watering can holds 5 gallons of water. How many gallons of water will Zane need to fill all 7 watering cans?

_____

$54 \div 6 = 9$

Write a related multiplication sentence.

_____

$70 \times 5 = $ _____

$70 \times 3 = $ _____

$50 \times 9 = $ _____

Show two ways to solve this problem.

$5 \times 5 \times 4$

Quan has 24 golf clubs. He has 3 golf bags. Each of the bags contains the same number of clubs. How many golf clubs are in each bag?

_____

**Day 3**

$847 - 358 = $

$6 \times $ _____ $= 42$

_____ $\times 9 = 45$

$9 \times 9 = $ _____

**Day 4**

Mr. Vale buys 48 flowers. He puts bunches of 6 flowers each in vases. If he sells each vase for $2, how much does he earn?

_____

$63 \div 9 = $ _____

$18 \div 9 = $ _____

$32 \div 4 = $ _____

$18 \div $ _____ $= 2$

_____ $\div 6 = 7$

$36 \div 4 = $ _____

A store's jar of jawbreakers has 50 pieces. Five customers buy equal numbers of jawbreakers until the jar is empty. How many pieces did each customer buy?

_____

Round each number to the nearest 10. Then, subtract.

$453 - 110$ is about

_____

Complete the table.

| Multiply by 9 | |
| --- | --- |
| 1 | 9 |
| 2 | |
| 3 | |
| 4 | |
| 5 | |

© Carson-Dellosa • CD-104592

Name_____

1.  70 × 7 = _____

    40 × 8 = _____

    30 × 5 = _____

2.  Catherine had 15 golf balls to put into buckets. She put 5 golf balls into each bucket. How many buckets did Catherine use?

    _____

3.  A case of candy bars contains 99 bars. There are 9 boxes in a case. How many candy bars are in each box?

    _____

4.  Complete the table.

| Multiply by 9 | |
| --- | --- |
| 5 | 45 |
| 6 | |
| 7 | |
| 8 | |
| 9 | |

5.  27 ÷ 3 = 9

    Write a related multiplication sentence.

    _____

6.  Show two ways to solve this problem.

    6 × 2 × 6

7.  _____ ÷ 8 = 6

    25 ÷ _____ = 5

    21 ÷ 3 = _____

8.  Mackenzie buys 6 petunias and 8 marigolds. If she plants 2 flowers in each pot, how many pots does she need?

    _____

9.  The iguanas in the reptile house eat 3 times per week. How many times will Ramsey need to feed the iguanas in the next 32 weeks?

    _____

10. _____ × 6 = 18

    7 × _____ = 42

    8 × 2 = _____

Name_____

**Day 1**

Divide this circle into fourths. Label each fourth with the appropriate fraction.

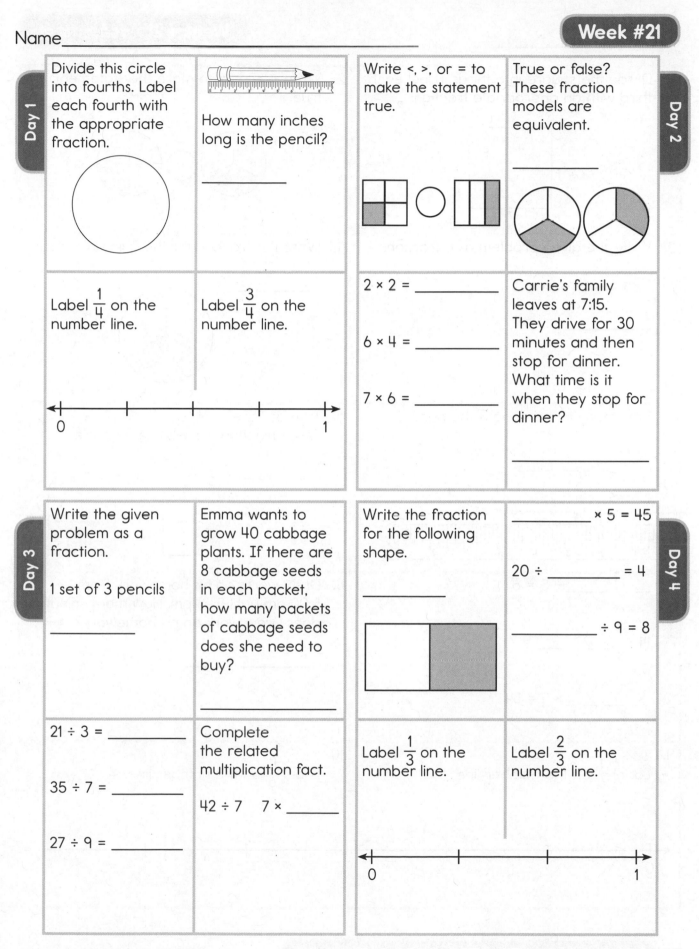

How many inches long is the pencil?

_____

Label $\frac{1}{4}$ on the number line.

Label $\frac{3}{4}$ on the number line.

0 ———————————— 1

**Day 2**

Write <, >, or = to make the statement true.

True or false? These fraction models are equivalent.

_____

$2 \times 2 =$ _____

$6 \times 4 =$ _____

$7 \times 6 =$ _____

Carrie's family leaves at 7:15. They drive for 30 minutes and then stop for dinner. What time is it when they stop for dinner?

_____

**Day 3**

Write the given problem as a fraction.

1 set of 3 pencils

_____

Emma wants to grow 40 cabbage plants. If there are 8 cabbage seeds in each packet, how many packets of cabbage seeds does she need to buy?

_____

$21 \div 3 =$ _____

$35 \div 7 =$ _____

$27 \div 9 =$ _____

Complete the related multiplication fact.

$42 \div 7 \quad 7 \times$ _____

**Day 4**

Write the fraction for the following shape.

_____

_____ $\times 5 = 45$

$20 \div$ _____ $= 4$

_____ $\div 9 = 8$

Label $\frac{1}{3}$ on the number line.

Label $\frac{2}{3}$ on the number line.

0 ———————————— 1

1. Divide the square into thirds. Label each third with an appropriate fraction.

2. Write <, >, or = to make the statement true.

3. Write the given problem as a fraction.

   1 set of 6 erasers

   _____

4. Write the fraction for the following shape.

   _____

5. How many inches long is this pen?

   _____

6. True or false?
   These fraction models are equivalent.

   _____

7. _____ ÷ 5 = 6

   14 ÷ _____ = 7

   _____ × 9 = 54

8. Drew works on his homework from 5:00 pm until 5:45 pm. How many minutes does Drew work on his homework?

   _____

9. Label $\frac{1}{6}$ on the number line.

10. Label $\frac{4}{6}$ on the number line.

0                                                1

3.OA.4, 3.NF.1, 3.NF.2, 3.NF.3, 3.MD.1, 3.MD.4, 3.G.2      CD-104592 • © Carson-Dellosa

Name_____

**Day 1**

Write the given problem as a fraction.

1 set of 7 daffodils

_____

In 7 days, Dylan jumped a total of 35 times. He jumped the same number of times each day. How many times did Dylan jump each day?

_____

477 + 298 =

Complete the fraction for the following shape.

$\frac{\phantom{0}}{6}$

**Day 2**

Round each number to the nearest 100.

502 − 321 is about

_____

If you multiply me by 7, add 1, and then divide by 4, you get 9. What number am I?

_____

Label $\frac{1}{8}$ on the number line.

Label $\frac{5}{8}$ on the number line.

```
|---+---+---+---+---+---+---+---|
0                               1
```

**Day 3**

How many inches long is the paintbrush?

_____

70 × 6 = _____

50 × 9 = _____

80 × 2 = _____

Write the appropriate fraction on the blank fraction bar.

```
|---+---+---+---+---+---|
0   1   2   _   4   5   1
    6   6       6   6
            1
            2
```

**Day 4**

Divide the rectangle into sixths. Label each sixth with the appropriate fraction.

In the evening, Lynn helps set up camp. There are 3 rows with 8 tents in each row. How many tents are there?

_____

True or false? The fractions $\frac{1}{2}$ and $\frac{3}{6}$ are equal.

_____

8 × 3 = _____

9 × 1 = _____

4 × 5 = _____

Write <, >, or = to make the statement true.

Name_____

1.  Write the given problem as a fraction.

    1 set of 5 shovels

    _____

2.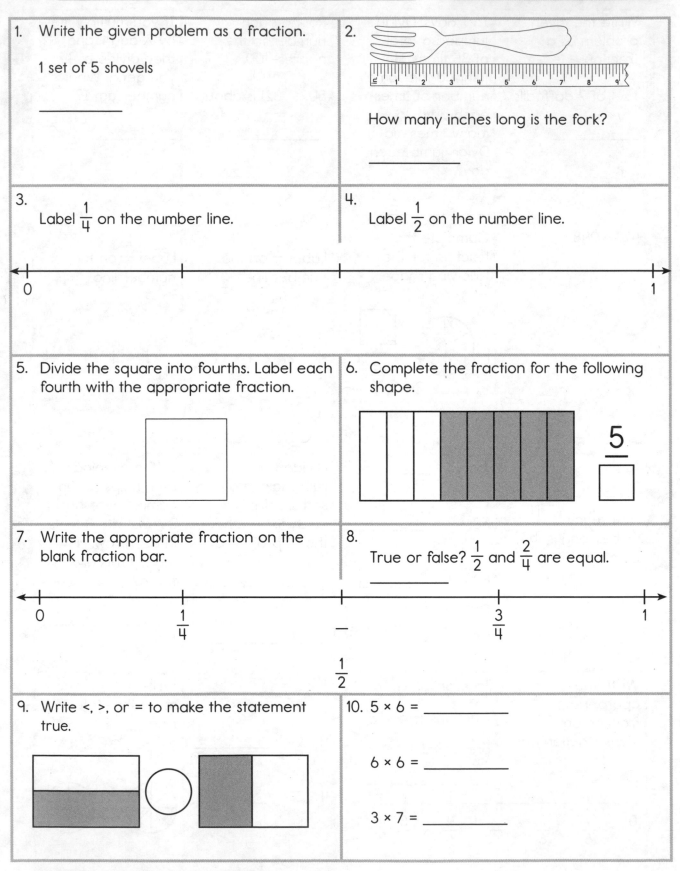

    How many inches long is the fork?

    _____

3.  Label $\frac{1}{4}$ on the number line.

4.  Label $\frac{1}{2}$ on the number line.

    0                                                                    1

5.  Divide the square into fourths. Label each fourth with the appropriate fraction.

6.  Complete the fraction for the following shape.

    $\dfrac{5}{\boxed{\phantom{0}}}$

7.  Write the appropriate fraction on the blank fraction bar.

    0            $\frac{1}{4}$            —            $\frac{3}{4}$            1

                                         $\frac{1}{2}$

8.  True or false? $\frac{1}{2}$ and $\frac{2}{4}$ are equal.

    _____

9.  Write <, >, or = to make the statement true.

10. 5 × 6 = _____

    6 × 6 = _____

    3 × 7 = _____

 3.OA.7, 3.NF.1, 3.NF.2, 3.NF.3, 3.MD.4, 3.G.2          CD-104592 • © Carson-Dellosa

Name_____

**Day 1**

Write the fraction for the following shape.

_____

Write the missing numbers to complete the pattern.
3, 6, 12,

_____,

_____,

_____

How many inches long is the paper clip?

_____

$12 \div 4 =$ _____

$10 \div 5 =$ _____

$9 \times 6 =$ _____

**Day 2**

Divide the circle into halves. Label each half with the appropriate fraction.

William ran a total of 14 miles in 7 days. Each day, he ran the same number of miles. How many miles did William run each day?

_____

$= \dfrac{\boxed{\phantom{0}}}{4}$

Brianna woke up at 1:10 am and was awake until 1:45 am. How many minutes was Brianna awake for?

_____

**Day 3**

Roxanne had 29 colorful rubber bands. Tyrone gave her some more. If Roxanne was able to give 6 friends 8 rubber bands each, how many rubber bands did Tyrone give her?

_____

$30 \div$ _____ $= 6$

_____ $\times 9 = 54$

$3 \times 5 =$ _____

Label $\dfrac{2}{6}$ on the number line.

0                                        1

Label $\dfrac{5}{6}$ on the number line.

**Day 4**

Show two ways to solve this problem.

$8 \times 2 \times 4$

Complete the related multiplication facts.

$12 \div 2$      $2 \times$ _____

$9 \div 3$      $3 \times$ _____

Write <, >, or = to make the statement true.

True or false? The fractions $\dfrac{1}{2}$ and $\dfrac{4}{8}$ are equal.

_____

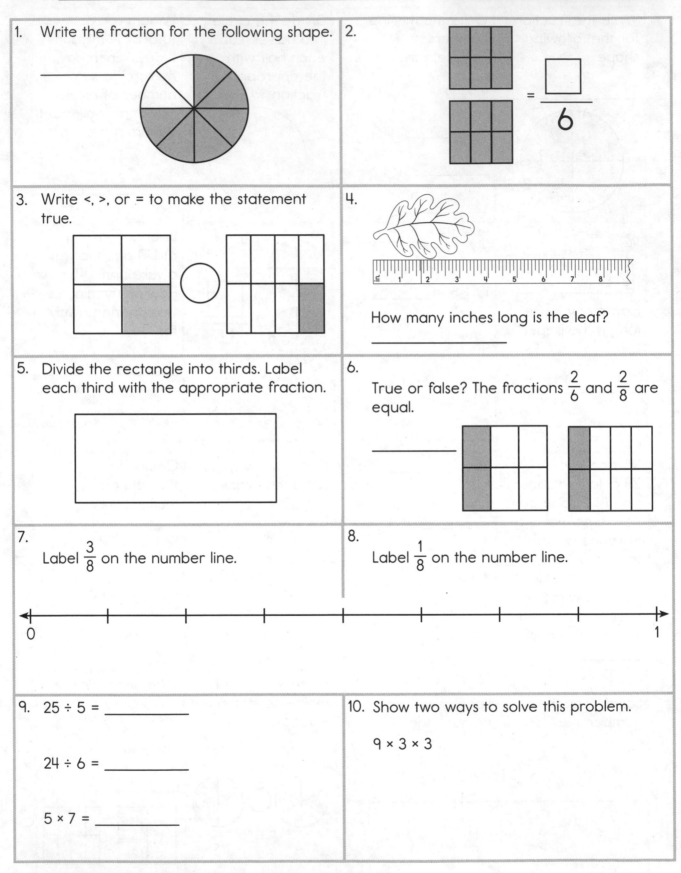

1. Write the fraction for the following shape.

   _____

2.

   = $\dfrac{\square}{6}$

3. Write <, >, or = to make the statement true.

4.

   How many inches long is the leaf?

   _____

5. Divide the rectangle into thirds. Label each third with the appropriate fraction.

6.

   True or false? The fractions $\dfrac{2}{6}$ and $\dfrac{2}{8}$ are equal.

   _____

7. Label $\dfrac{3}{8}$ on the number line.

8. Label $\dfrac{1}{8}$ on the number line.

   0                                                    1

9. $25 \div 5 =$ _____

   $24 \div 6 =$ _____

   $5 \times 7 =$ _____

10. Show two ways to solve this problem.

   $9 \times 3 \times 3$

3.OA.5, 3.OA.7, 3.NF.1, 3.NF.2, 3.NF.3, 3.MD.4, 3.G.2        CD-104592 • © Carson-Dellosa

Name_____

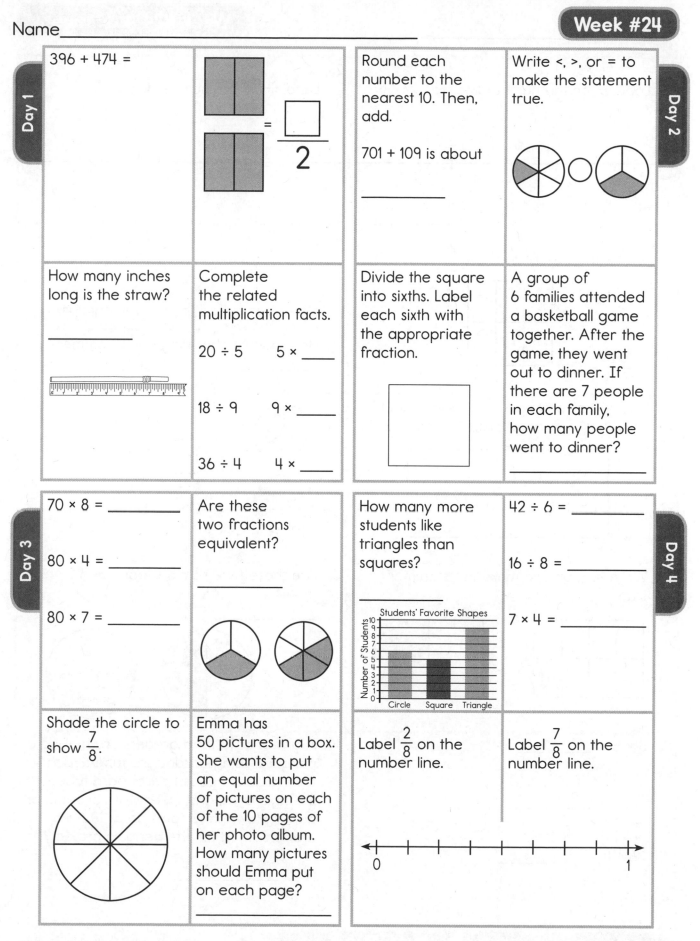

**Day 1**

396 + 474 =

= □/2

How many inches long is the straw?

_____

Complete the related multiplication facts.

20 ÷ 5        5 × ____

18 ÷ 9        9 × ____

36 ÷ 4        4 × ____

**Day 2**

Round each number to the nearest 10. Then, add.

701 + 109 is about

_____

Write <, >, or = to make the statement true.

Divide the square into sixths. Label each sixth with the appropriate fraction.

A group of 6 families attended a basketball game together. After the game, they went out to dinner. If there are 7 people in each family, how many people went to dinner?

_____

**Day 3**

70 × 8 = _____

80 × 4 = _____

80 × 7 = _____

Are these two fractions equivalent?

_____

Shade the circle to show $\frac{7}{8}$.

Emma has 50 pictures in a box. She wants to put an equal number of pictures on each of the 10 pages of her photo album. How many pictures should Emma put on each page?

_____

**Day 4**

How many more students like triangles than squares?

_____

Students' Favorite Shapes
Number of Students
Circle    Square    Triangle

42 ÷ 6 = _____

16 ÷ 8 = _____

7 × 4 = _____

Label $\frac{2}{8}$ on the number line.

Label $\frac{7}{8}$ on the number line.

0                    1

Name_____

1. Label $\frac{3}{6}$ on the number line.

2. Label $\frac{6}{6}$ on the number line.

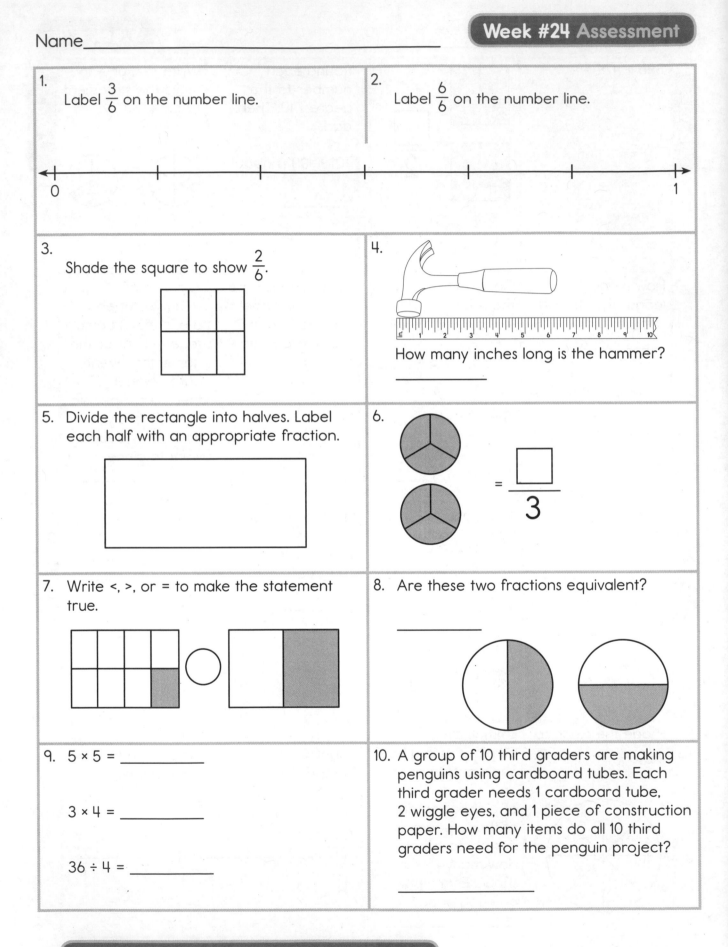

0                                                            1

3. Shade the square to show $\frac{2}{6}$.

4. How many inches long is the hammer?
_____

5. Divide the rectangle into halves. Label each half with an appropriate fraction.

6. $= \dfrac{\boxed{\phantom{0}}}{3}$

7. Write <, >, or = to make the statement true.

8. Are these two fractions equivalent?
_____

9. $5 \times 5 =$ _____

   $3 \times 4 =$ _____

   $36 \div 4 =$ _____

10. A group of 10 third graders are making penguins using cardboard tubes. Each third grader needs 1 cardboard tube, 2 wiggle eyes, and 1 piece of construction paper. How many items do all 10 third graders need for the penguin project?

_____

3.OA.7, 3.OA.8, 3.NF.1, 3.NF.2, 3.NF.3, 3.MD.4, 3.G.2    CD-104592 • © Carson-Dellosa

Name_____

**Day 1**

In 4 days, Paige saw a total of 32 skydivers. She saw the same number of skydivers each day. How many skydivers did Paige see in one day?

_____

_____ ÷ 2 = 5

1 × _____ = 9

42 ÷ 7 = _____

**Day 2**

Tavaris has 2 pairs of pants hanging in his closet. Each pair of pants has 2 pockets. How many pockets are there in all?

_____

Divide the circle into thirds and shade the pieces to show $\frac{2}{3}$.

Label $\frac{4}{8}$ on the number line.

Label $\frac{6}{8}$ on the number line.

0                1

Write <, >, or = to make the statement true.

Complete the related multiplication facts.

24 ÷ 8      8 × ____

42 ÷ 6      6 × ____

16 ÷ 4      4 × ____

**Day 3**

Valerie has 59 scarves in her closet. In all, 14 of the scarves are red, 29 of the scarves are striped, and the remaining scarves are white. How many of Valerie's scarves are white?

_____

Are these two fractions equivalent? _____

**Day 4**

4 × 3 = _____

4 × 9 = _____

48 ÷ 6 = _____

= [ ] / 8

How many inches wide is the butterfly?

_____

Round each number to the nearest 100.

780 – 644 is about

_____

Divide the rectangle into fourths. Label each fourth with the appropriate fraction.

Write the missing numbers to complete the pattern.
56, 64, 72,

_____,

_____,

_____

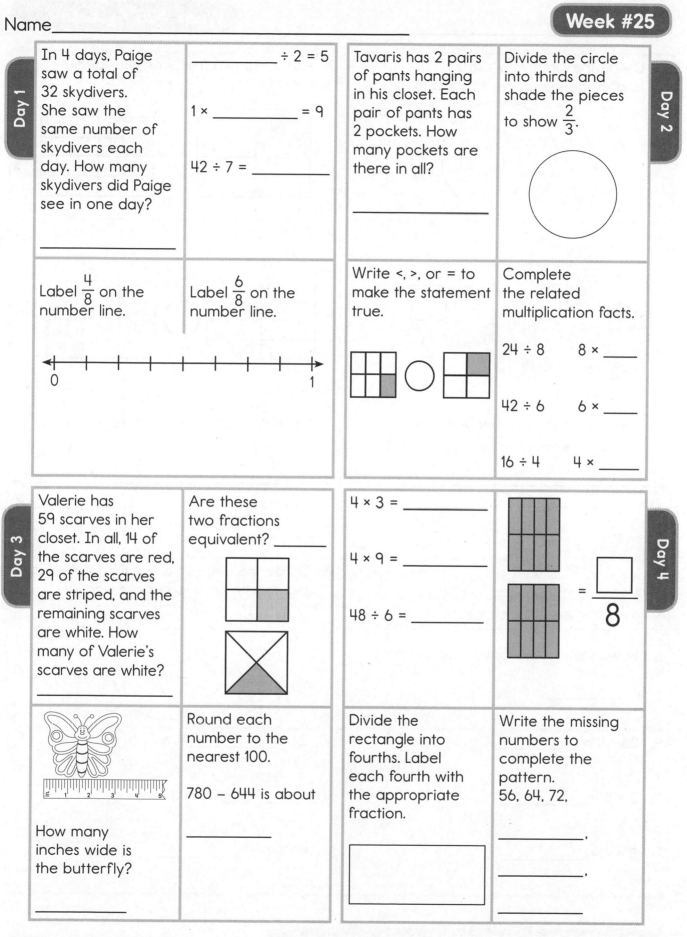

Name_____

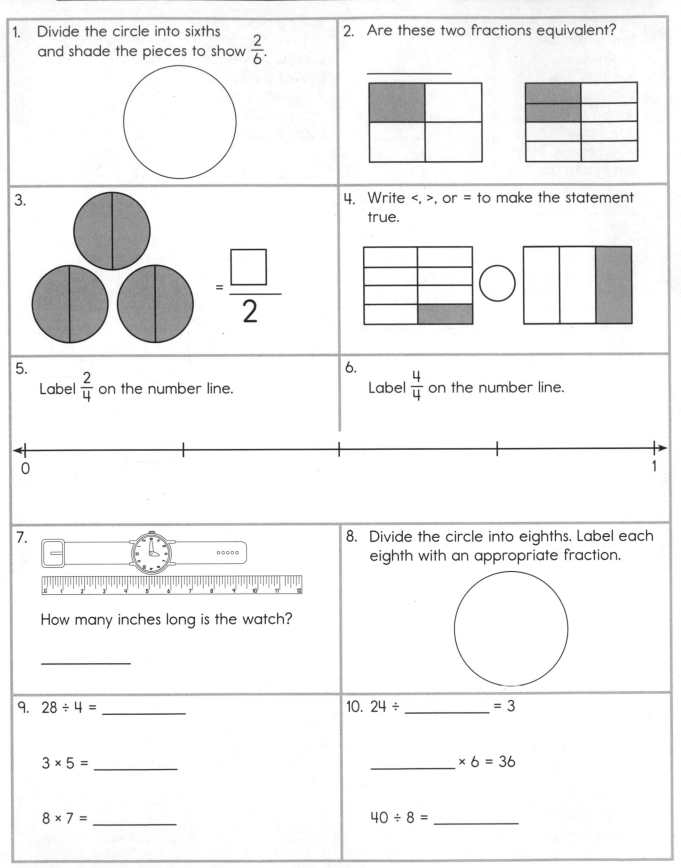

1.  Divide the circle into sixths and shade the pieces to show $\frac{2}{6}$.

2.  Are these two fractions equivalent?

    _____

3.  $= \dfrac{\square}{2}$

4.  Write <, >, or = to make the statement true.

5.  Label $\frac{2}{4}$ on the number line.

6.  Label $\frac{4}{4}$ on the number line.

    0                                                                      1

7.  How many inches long is the watch?

    _____

8.  Divide the circle into eighths. Label each eighth with an appropriate fraction.

9.  28 ÷ 4 = _____

    3 × 5 = _____

    8 × 7 = _____

10. 24 ÷ _____ = 3

    _____ × 6 = 36

    40 ÷ 8 = _____

3.OA.4, 3.OA.7, 3.NF.1, 3.NF.2, 3.NF.3, 3.MD.4, 3.G.2          CD-104592 • © Carson-Dellosa

Name_____

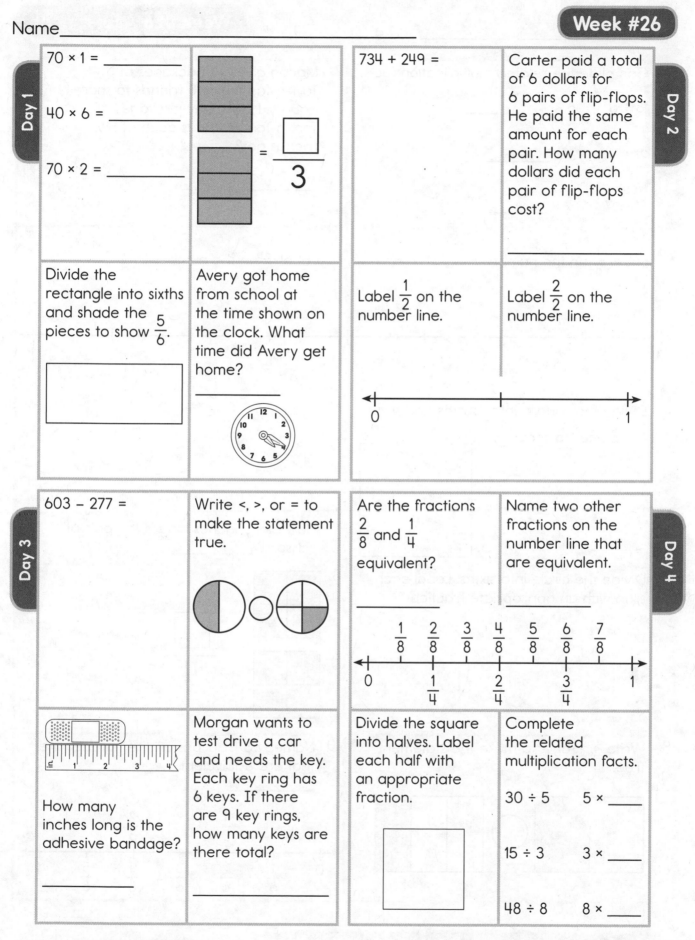

**Day 1**

70 × 1 = _____

40 × 6 = _____

70 × 2 = _____

$= \dfrac{\boxed{\phantom{0}}}{3}$

Divide the rectangle into sixths and shade the pieces to show $\frac{5}{6}$.

Avery got home from school at the time shown on the clock. What time did Avery get home?

_____

**Day 2**

734 + 249 =

Carter paid a total of 6 dollars for 6 pairs of flip-flops. He paid the same amount for each pair. How many dollars did each pair of flip-flops cost?

_____

Label $\frac{1}{2}$ on the number line.

Label $\frac{2}{2}$ on the number line.

0                              1

**Day 3**

603 – 277 =

Write <, >, or = to make the statement true.

How many inches long is the adhesive bandage?

_____

Morgan wants to test drive a car and needs the key. Each key ring has 6 keys. If there are 9 key rings, how many keys are there total?

_____

**Day 4**

Are the fractions $\frac{2}{8}$ and $\frac{1}{4}$ equivalent?

_____

Name two other fractions on the number line that are equivalent.

_____

$\frac{1}{8}$  $\frac{2}{8}$  $\frac{3}{8}$  $\frac{4}{8}$  $\frac{5}{8}$  $\frac{6}{8}$  $\frac{7}{8}$

0     $\frac{1}{4}$     $\frac{2}{4}$     $\frac{3}{4}$     1

Divide the square into halves. Label each half with an appropriate fraction.

Complete the related multiplication facts.

30 ÷ 5      5 × _____

15 ÷ 3      3 × _____

48 ÷ 8      8 × _____

1. Complete the related multiplication facts.

   18 ÷ 6      6 × _____

   21 ÷ 3      3 × _____

   35 ÷ 7      7 × _____

2. Macon gives 72 packages of Tart-n-Tangies to 8 friends to share equally. How many packages of Tart-n-Tangies does each of his friends get?

   _____

3. Label $\frac{1}{8}$ on the number line.

4. Label $\frac{8}{8}$ on the number line.

0 —————————————————————— 1

5. Divide the square into fourths and shade the pieces to show $\frac{2}{4}$.

6. How many inches long is the pair of scissors? _____

7. Divide the circle into sixths. Label each sixth with an appropriate fraction.

8. $= \dfrac{\boxed{\phantom{0}}}{4}$

9. Write <, >, or = to make the statement true.

10. Name two fractions on the number line that are equivalent.

    _____

    $\frac{1}{3}$        $\frac{2}{3}$

    0    $\frac{1}{6}$    $\frac{2}{6}$    $\frac{3}{6}$    $\frac{4}{6}$    $\frac{5}{6}$    1

3.OA.3, 3.OA.6, 3.NF.1, 3.NF.2, 3.NF.3, 3.MD.4, 3.G.2        CD-104592 • © Carson-Dellosa

Name_____

**Day 1**

$32 \div 8 =$ _____

$18 \div 3 =$ _____

$5 \times 3 =$ _____

Divide this square into eighths. Label each eighth with an appropriate fraction.

Are the fractions $\frac{1}{2}$ and $\frac{3}{4}$ equivalent?

_____

Name two fractions on the number line that are equivalent.

_____

**Day 2**

There were 21 skiers waiting in line to get on the ski lift. Three skiers can sit on each seat on the lift. How many seats are needed for all of the skiers?

_____

Use the information below to fill in the line plot.

$4 \frac{1}{4}$ in. = 5
$4 \frac{1}{2}$ in. = 6
$5 \frac{1}{4}$ in. = 3

**Paintbrushes in the Art Room**

$5 \times 2 \times 1 =$ _____

Divide the circle into sixths and shade the pieces to show $\frac{3}{6}$.

**Day 3**

Jayla found 11 starfish. Each starfish had 5 arms. How many arms did the starfish have in all?

_____

Write <, >, or = to make the statement true.

Divide this number line into fourths.

Label the fractions $\frac{1}{4}$ and $\frac{3}{4}$.

**Day 4**

Complete the related multiplication facts.

$32 \div 4$      $4 \times$ ____

$20 \div 5$      $5 \times$ ____

$24 \div 6$      $6 \times$ ____

= $\frac{\square}{6}$

Janelle has 91 erasers, and Greg gives her 8 more. Janelle gives each of the 9 friends at her party an equal number of erasers. How many erasers will each friend get?

_____

Round each number to the nearest 10. Then, subtract.

867 – 345 is about

_____

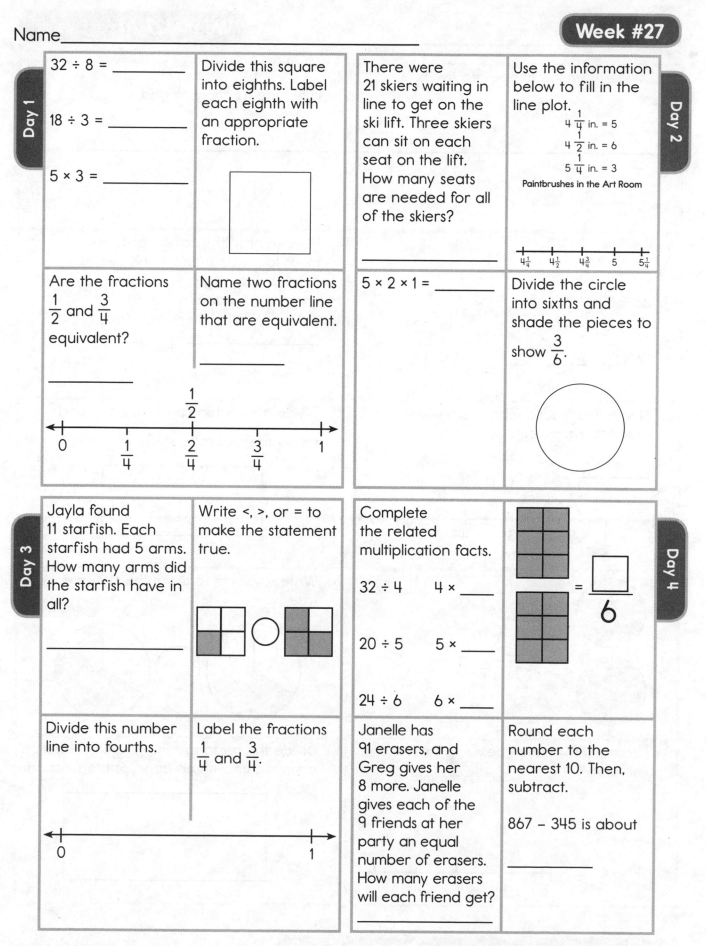

Name_____

1. Divide the number line into thirds.

2. Label the fractions $\frac{1}{3}$ and $\frac{2}{3}$.

0 ———————————————————————— 1

3. $5 \times 9 =$ _____

   $35 \div 5 =$ _____

   $36 \div 9 =$ _____

4. Hayden has 90 trading cards. He plans to divide them evenly between 10 mounting pages. How many cards will go on each page?

   _____

5. Name two fractions on the number line that are equivalent.

   _____

   $\frac{1}{2}$

   0   $\frac{1}{6}$   $\frac{2}{6}$   $\frac{3}{6}$   $\frac{4}{6}$   $\frac{5}{6}$   1

6. Divide the rectangle into eighths and shade the pieces to show $\frac{2}{8}$.

7.

   $= \dfrac{\boxed{\phantom{0}}}{2}$

8. Write <, >, or = to make the statement true.

9. Use the information below to fill in the line plot.

   **Sticks in the Yard**

   $10\frac{1}{2}$ in. = 3

   $11\frac{1}{4}$ in. = 1

   $11\frac{1}{2}$ in. = 5

   $10\frac{1}{2}$   $10\frac{3}{4}$   11   $11\frac{1}{4}$   $11\frac{1}{2}$

10. Divide this rectangle into eighths. Label each eighth with an appropriate fraction.

3.OA.3, 3.OA.7, 3.NF.1, 3.NF.2, 3.NF.3, 3.MD.4, 3.G.2 CD-104592 • © Carson-Dellosa

Name_____

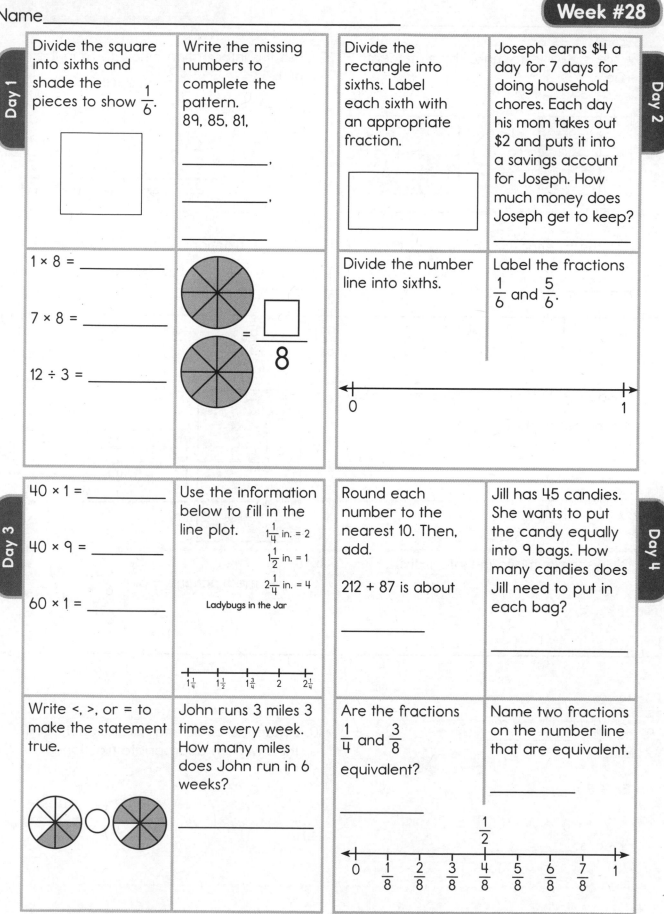

**Day 1**

Divide the square into sixths and shade the pieces to show $\frac{1}{6}$.

Write the missing numbers to complete the pattern.
89, 85, 81,

_____ ,

_____ ,

_____

$1 \times 8 =$ _____

$7 \times 8 =$ _____

$12 \div 3 =$ _____

= $\dfrac{\boxed{\phantom{8}}}{8}$

**Day 2**

Divide the rectangle into sixths. Label each sixth with an appropriate fraction.

Joseph earns $4 a day for 7 days for doing household chores. Each day his mom takes out $2 and puts it into a savings account for Joseph. How much money does Joseph get to keep?

_____

Divide the number line into sixths.

Label the fractions $\frac{1}{6}$ and $\frac{5}{6}$.

0 ————————————— 1

**Day 3**

$40 \times 1 =$ _____

$40 \times 9 =$ _____

$60 \times 1 =$ _____

Use the information below to fill in the line plot.

$1\frac{1}{4}$ in. = 2

$1\frac{1}{2}$ in. = 1

$2\frac{1}{4}$ in. = 4

Ladybugs in the Jar

$1\frac{1}{4}$  $1\frac{1}{2}$  $1\frac{3}{4}$  2  $2\frac{1}{4}$

**Day 4**

Round each number to the nearest 10. Then, add.

$212 + 87$ is about

_____

Jill has 45 candies. She wants to put the candy equally into 9 bags. How many candies does Jill need to put in each bag?

_____

Write <, >, or = to make the statement true.

◯ ◯ ◯

John runs 3 miles 3 times every week. How many miles does John run in 6 weeks?

_____

Are the fractions $\frac{1}{4}$ and $\frac{3}{8}$ equivalent?

_____

Name two fractions on the number line that are equivalent.

_____

$\frac{1}{2}$

0  $\frac{1}{8}$  $\frac{2}{8}$  $\frac{3}{8}$  $\frac{4}{8}$  $\frac{5}{8}$  $\frac{6}{8}$  $\frac{7}{8}$  1

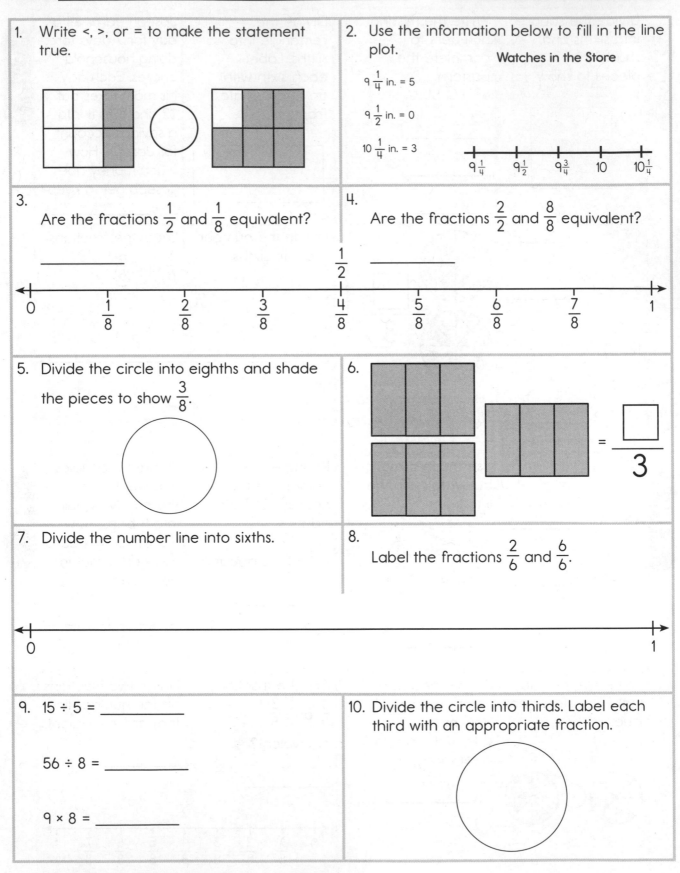

1. Write <, >, or = to make the statement true.

2. Use the information below to fill in the line plot.

   **Watches in the Store**

   $9\frac{1}{4}$ in. = 5

   $9\frac{1}{2}$ in. = 0

   $10\frac{1}{4}$ in. = 3

3. Are the fractions $\frac{1}{2}$ and $\frac{1}{8}$ equivalent?

   _____

4. Are the fractions $\frac{2}{2}$ and $\frac{8}{8}$ equivalent?

   _____

5. Divide the circle into eighths and shade the pieces to show $\frac{3}{8}$.

6. $= \dfrac{\square}{3}$

7. Divide the number line into sixths.

8. Label the fractions $\frac{2}{6}$ and $\frac{6}{6}$.

9. $15 \div 5 =$ _____

   $56 \div 8 =$ _____

   $9 \times 8 =$ _____

10. Divide the circle into thirds. Label each third with an appropriate fraction.

3.OA.7, 3.NF.1, 3.NF.2, 3.NF.3, 3.MD.4, 3.G.2     CD-104592 • © Carson-Dellosa

Name_____

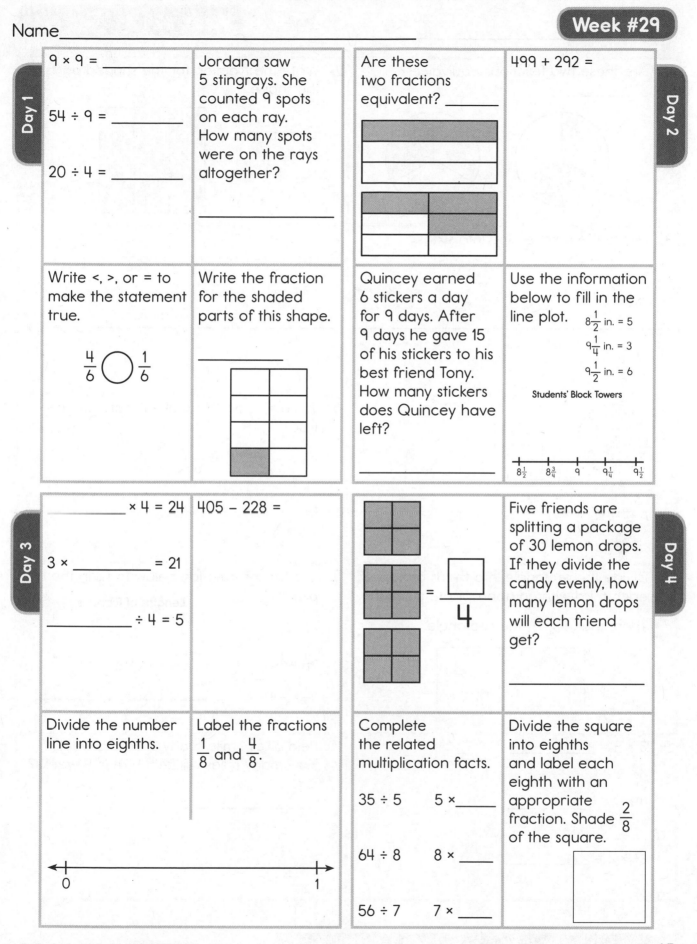

**Day 1**

$9 \times 9 =$ _____

$54 \div 9 =$ _____

$20 \div 4 =$ _____

Jordana saw 5 stingrays. She counted 9 spots on each ray. How many spots were on the rays altogether?

_____

Write <, >, or = to make the statement true.

$\frac{4}{6} \bigcirc \frac{1}{6}$

Write the fraction for the shaded parts of this shape.

_____

**Day 2**

Are these two fractions equivalent? _____

$499 + 292 =$

Quincey earned 6 stickers a day for 9 days. After 9 days he gave 15 of his stickers to his best friend Tony. How many stickers does Quincey have left?

_____

Use the information below to fill in the line plot.

$8\frac{1}{2}$ in. = 5

$9\frac{1}{4}$ in. = 3

$9\frac{1}{2}$ in. = 6

Students' Block Towers

$8\frac{1}{2}$  $8\frac{3}{4}$  $9$  $9\frac{1}{4}$  $9\frac{1}{2}$

**Day 3**

_____ $\times 4 = 24$

$3 \times$ _____ $= 21$

_____ $\div 4 = 5$

$405 - 228 =$

Divide the number line into eighths.

0 _____ 1

Label the fractions $\frac{1}{8}$ and $\frac{4}{8}$.

**Day 4**

$= \dfrac{\boxed{\phantom{0}}}{4}$

Five friends are splitting a package of 30 lemon drops. If they divide the candy evenly, how many lemon drops will each friend get?

_____

Complete the related multiplication facts.

$35 \div 5$    $5 \times$ _____

$64 \div 8$    $8 \times$ _____

$56 \div 7$    $7 \times$ _____

Divide the square into eighths and label each eighth with an appropriate fraction. Shade $\frac{2}{8}$ of the square.

Name_____

1. Are these two fractions equivalent?

   _____

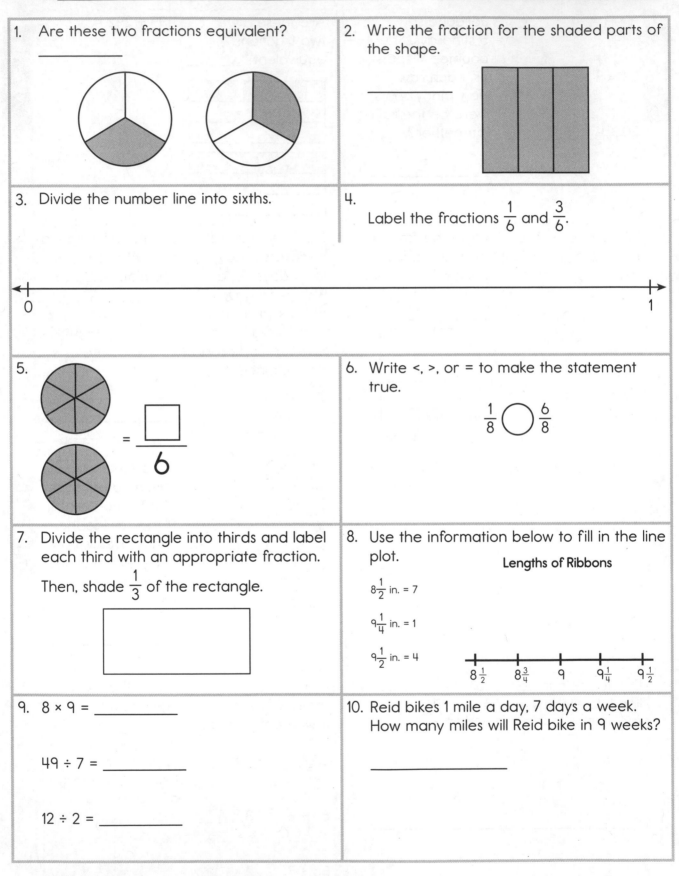

2. Write the fraction for the shaded parts of the shape.

   _____

3. Divide the number line into sixths.

4. Label the fractions $\frac{1}{6}$ and $\frac{3}{6}$.

   0 |——————————————————————| 1

5. = $\frac{\square}{6}$

6. Write <, >, or = to make the statement true.

   $\frac{1}{8}$ ◯ $\frac{6}{8}$

7. Divide the rectangle into thirds and label each third with an appropriate fraction.

   Then, shade $\frac{1}{3}$ of the rectangle.

8. Use the information below to fill in the line plot.

   **Lengths of Ribbons**

   $8\frac{1}{2}$ in. = 7

   $9\frac{1}{4}$ in. = 1

   $9\frac{1}{2}$ in. = 4

   $8\frac{1}{2}$   $8\frac{3}{4}$   9   $9\frac{1}{4}$   $9\frac{1}{2}$

9. 8 × 9 = _____

   49 ÷ 7 = _____

   12 ÷ 2 = _____

10. Reid bikes 1 mile a day, 7 days a week. How many miles will Reid bike in 9 weeks?

    _____

3.OA.7, 3.OA.8, 3.NF.1, 3.NF.2, 3.NF.3, 3.MD.4, 3.G.2     CD-104592 • © Carson-Dellosa

Name_____

**Day 1**

Look at the clock. Blair arrived at the bus stop 45 minutes ago. What time did Blair arrive at the bus stop?

_____

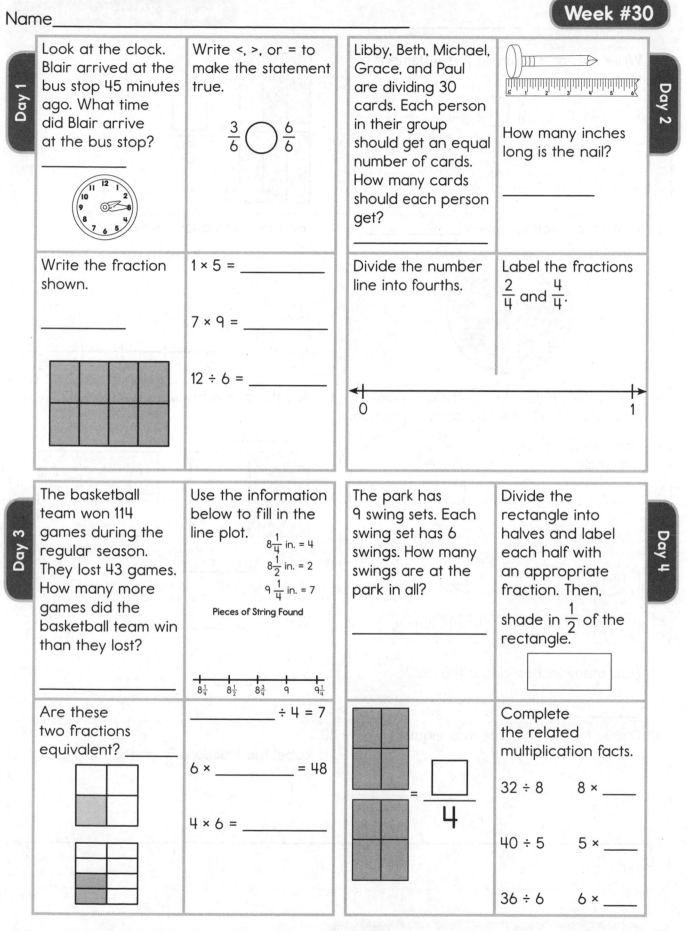

Write <, >, or = to make the statement true.

$\frac{3}{6}$ ◯ $\frac{6}{6}$

**Day 2**

Libby, Beth, Michael, Grace, and Paul are dividing 30 cards. Each person in their group should get an equal number of cards. How many cards should each person get?

_____

How many inches long is the nail?

_____

Write the fraction shown.

_____

$1 \times 5 =$ _____

$7 \times 9 =$ _____

$12 \div 6 =$ _____

Divide the number line into fourths.

Label the fractions $\frac{2}{4}$ and $\frac{4}{4}$.

0 ———————————— 1

**Day 3**

The basketball team won 114 games during the regular season. They lost 43 games. How many more games did the basketball team win than they lost?

_____

Use the information below to fill in the line plot.

$8\frac{1}{4}$ in. = 4
$8\frac{1}{2}$ in. = 2
$9\frac{1}{4}$ in. = 7

**Pieces of String Found**

$8\frac{1}{4}$  $8\frac{1}{2}$  $8\frac{3}{4}$  $9$  $9\frac{1}{4}$

**Day 4**

The park has 9 swing sets. Each swing set has 6 swings. How many swings are at the park in all?

_____

Divide the rectangle into halves and label each half with an appropriate fraction. Then, shade in $\frac{1}{2}$ of the rectangle.

Are these two fractions equivalent? _____

_____ ÷ 4 = 7

$6 \times$ _____ = 48

$4 \times 6 =$ _____

$=\frac{\boxed{\phantom{0}}}{4}$

Complete the related multiplication facts.

$32 \div 8$      $8 \times$ ____

$40 \div 5$      $5 \times$ ____

$36 \div 6$      $6 \times$ ____

Name_____

1. Write <, >, or = to make the statement true.

$\frac{2}{8}$ ◯ $\frac{8}{8}$

2.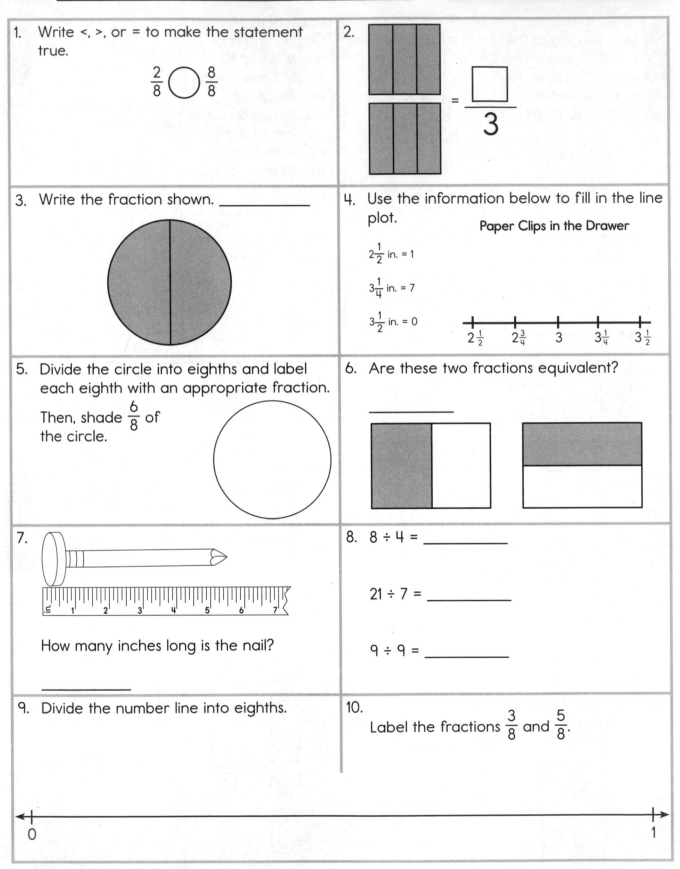

$= \dfrac{\Box}{3}$

3. Write the fraction shown. _____

4. Use the information below to fill in the line plot.

**Paper Clips in the Drawer**

$2\frac{1}{2}$ in. = 1

$3\frac{1}{4}$ in. = 7

$3\frac{1}{2}$ in. = 0

$2\frac{1}{2}$  $2\frac{3}{4}$  $3$  $3\frac{1}{4}$  $3\frac{1}{2}$

5. Divide the circle into eighths and label each eighth with an appropriate fraction. Then, shade $\frac{6}{8}$ of the circle.

6. Are these two fractions equivalent?

_____

7. How many inches long is the nail?

_____

8. $8 \div 4 =$ _____

$21 \div 7 =$ _____

$9 \div 9 =$ _____

9. Divide the number line into eighths.

10. Label the fractions $\frac{3}{8}$ and $\frac{5}{8}$.

0                                                    1

 3.OA.7, 3.NF.1, 3.NF.2, 3.NF.3, 3.MD.4, 3.G.2     CD-104592 • © Carson-Dellosa

**Day 1**

Victor is going on a trip at 3:15. He needs 30 minutes to pack. What time does Victor need to start packing so that he will be ready to leave at 3:15?

_____

$9 \times 8 =$ _____

$16 \div 2 =$ _____

$2 \times 5 =$ _____

Henry has 3 baskets of apples. Each basket holds 2 apples. How many apples are there in all?

_____

Complete the related multiplication facts.

$24 \div 4$     $4 \times$ _____

$49 \div 7$     $7 \times$ _____

$16 \div 8$     $8 \times$ _____

**Day 2**

About how much water will a bucket hold?

A.  5 inches
B.  5 pounds
C.  5 liters
D.  5 ounces

$118 + 853 =$

Are these two fractions equivalent? _____

Round each number to the nearest 100. Then, add.

$153 + 117$ is about

_____

**Day 3**

What is the area of the rectangle?

_____ square units

$235 - 128 =$

Write <, >, or = to make the statement true.

$\frac{1}{4} \bigcirc \frac{2}{4}$

Write the fraction shown.

_____

**Day 4**

3 cm     3 cm

3 cm

What is the perimeter of the shape?

_____

John has 24 books to place equally on 4 shelves. How many books go on each shelf?

_____

Blane, Bobbi, and Brian combined all of their toy cars. Blane had 21, Bobbi had 35, and Brian had 16. They wanted to donate their toys to 9 friends. How many toy cars did each friend get?

_____

Write the missing numbers to finish the pattern.

97, 92, 87, _____,

_____,

_____

1. Kellie is going to the beach at 8:00. She needs to eat breakfast before she goes, and it takes her 45 minutes to eat. What time does Kellie need to start eating breakfast so that she will be ready to leave at 8:00?

_____

2. About how much does a pencil weigh?

   A. 2 grams
   B. 20 grams
   C. 200 grams
   D. 2,000 grams

3.

What is the area of the rectangle?

_____ square units

4.

5 cm

5 cm          5 cm

5 cm

What is the perimeter of the shape?

_____

5. $4 \times 6 =$ _____

   $5 \times 1 =$ _____

   $56 \div 7 =$ _____

6. $549 + 202 =$

7. Taron has 42 books and 7 shelves. How many books should he put on each shelf so that each shelf has an equal number of books?

_____

8. Write <, >, or = to make the statement true.

   $\frac{1}{8}$ $\bigcirc$ $\frac{4}{8}$

9. Callista read 35 pages of her book on Friday and 52 pages of her book on Saturday. If the book is 105 pages long, and Callista only has 2 more days to finish the book, how many pages must she read each day?

_____

10. Write the fraction shown.

   $\frac{6}{6}$

3.OA.3, 3.OA.7, 3.OA.8, 3.NBT.2, 3.NF.1, 3.NF.3, 3.MD.1, 3.MD.2, 3.MD.5, 3.MD.6, 3.MD.8      CD-104592 • © Carson-Dellosa

**Day 1**

_____ ÷ 2 = 7

5 × _____ = 30

8 × 6 = _____

Look at the clock. What time will it be in 25 minutes? _____

Round each number to the nearest 10. Then, subtract.

653 – 307 is about

_____

Henry found 79 shells on the beach. He gave his mom 34 shells. Later, Henry found 81 more shells. How many shells did Henry have now?

_____

**Day 2**

5 × 7 = 35

Write a related multiplication sentence.

_____

6 in.
2 in.          2 in.
6 in.

What is the perimeter of the shape?

_____

5 ÷ 1 = _____

8 × 8 = _____

36 ÷ 4 = _____

549 + 202 =

**Day 3**

Write the missing numbers to finish the pattern.

186, 180, 174,

_____ ,

_____ ,

_____

About how much does a refrigerator weigh?

A.   90 grams
B.   90 kilograms

834 – 657 =

Ian caught 4 fish during each hour that he fished. If he fished for 7 hours, how many fish did he catch?

_____

**Day 4**

20 × 1 = _____

70 × 4 = _____

80 × 6 = _____

Round each number to the nearest 10. Then, subtract.

748 – 259 is about

_____

What is the area of the rectangle?

_____ square units

A jar of 36 pickles will be divided equally between 4 people. How many pickles will each person get?

_____

1. _____ ÷ 5 = 8

   4 × _____ = 28

   3 × 4 = _____

2. 80 × 3 = _____

   20 × 9 = _____

   90 × 3 = _____

3. Wesley has 24 cars to put into 3 boxes. If he puts the same number of cars in each box, how many cars should go in a box?

   _____

4. How many more miles did Team 3 canoe than Teams 1 and 2 combined?

   _____

   **Miles Canoed**

   | Team 1 | 🛶🛶🛶 |
   | Team 2 | 🛶🛶 |
   | Team 3 | 🛶🛶🛶🛶🛶🛶🛶 |

   🛶 = 20 miles

5. Look at the clock. What time will it be in 50 minutes?

   _____

6. 

   2 in.    2 in.

   2 in.    2 in.

   2 in.

   What is the perimeter of this shape?

   _____

7. About how much does a wading pool hold?

   A. 500 grams
   B. 500 liters

8. 

   What is the area of the rectangle?

   _____ square units

9. 5 × 4 = _____

   4 × 8 = _____

   72 ÷ 8 = _____

10. A clam has 2 shells. How many shells do 6 clams have altogether?

    _____

 3.OA.3, 3.OA.4, 3.OA.7, 3.NBT.3, 3.MD.1, 3.MD.2, 3.MD.3, 3.MD.5, 3.MD.6, 3.MD.8   CD-104592 • © Carson-Dellosa

Name_____

**Day 1**

Write <, >, or = to make the statement true.

$$\frac{5}{8} \bigcirc \frac{1}{8}$$

Donna has 32 new CDs. Her CD carrier holds 4 CDs on each page. How many pages will she need to hold her CDs?

_____

Complete the related multiplication facts.

18 ÷ 3        3 × ____

20 ÷ 4        4 × ____

45 ÷ 9        9 × ____

**Day 2**

Jaime had 4 packages of stickers. Each package had 4 stickers in it. How many stickers did Jaime have?

_____

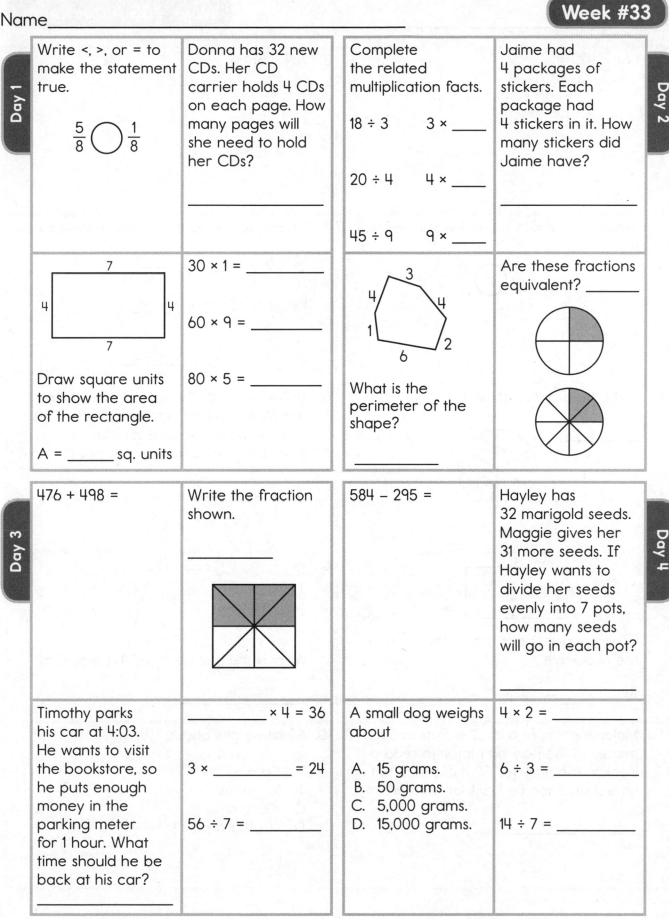

Draw square units to show the area of the rectangle.

A = _____ sq. units

30 × 1 = _____

60 × 9 = _____

80 × 5 = _____

What is the perimeter of the shape?

_____

Are these fractions equivalent? _____

**Day 3**

476 + 498 =

Write the fraction shown.

_____

584 − 295 =

**Day 4**

Hayley has 32 marigold seeds. Maggie gives her 31 more seeds. If Hayley wants to divide her seeds evenly into 7 pots, how many seeds will go in each pot?

_____

Timothy parks his car at 4:03. He wants to visit the bookstore, so he puts enough money in the parking meter for 1 hour. What time should he be back at his car?

_____

_____ × 4 = 36

3 × _____ = 24

56 ÷ 7 = _____

A small dog weighs about

A.  15 grams.
B.  50 grams.
C.  5,000 grams.
D.  15,000 grams.

4 × 2 = _____

6 ÷ 3 = _____

14 ÷ 7 = _____

| | |
|---|---|
| 1.  566 + 427 = | 2.  784 − 591 = |

3.  Write <, >, or = to make the statement true.

$$\frac{1}{2} \bigcirc \frac{2}{2}$$

4.  Complete the related multiplication facts.

48 ÷ 6      6 × _____

10 ÷ 2      2 × _____

63 ÷ 7      7 × _____

5.  Write the fraction shown.

_____

6.  Taylor earns $3 for washing the dishes and $2 for making her bed. If she does both of these chores each day for 5 days, how much money does she earn?

_____

7.

Draw square units to show the area of the rectangle.

A = _____ sq. units

8.

What is the perimeter of the shape?

_____

9.  Melanie parks at 6:25. She puts enough money in the parking meter to read a book in the park for 50 minutes. What time should she be back at her car?

_____

10. A nail weighs about

A.  1 gram.
B.  10 grams.
C.  100 grams.
D.  1,000 grams.

3.OA.6, 3.OA.8, 3.NBT.2, 3.NF.1, 3.NF.3, 3.MD.1, 3.MD.2, 3.MD.5, 3.MD.7, 3.MD.8 CD-104592 • © Carson-Dellosa

Name_____

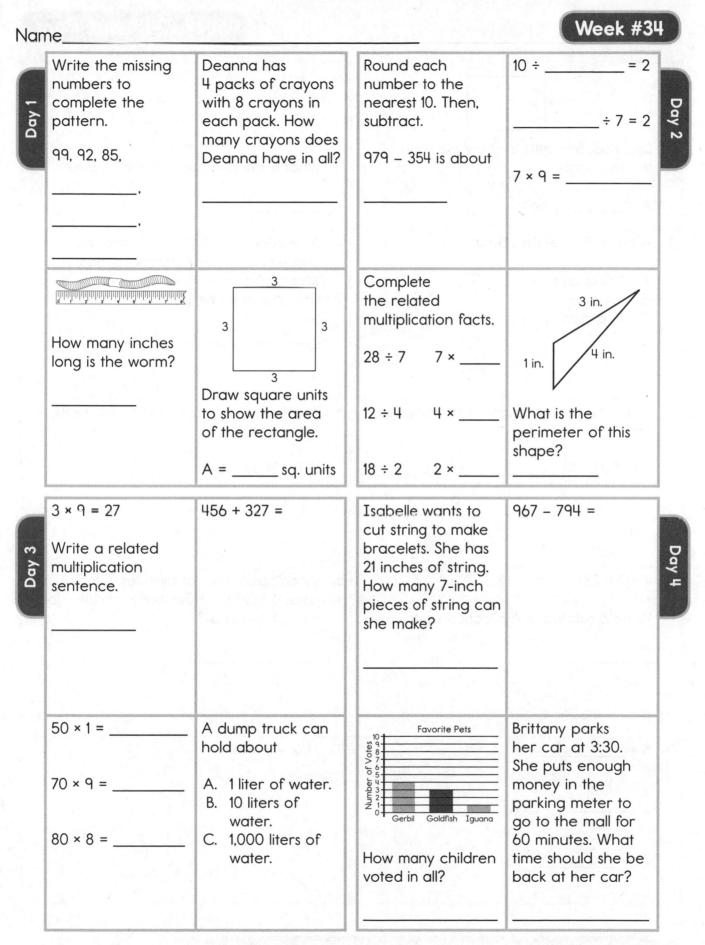

**Day 1**

Write the missing numbers to complete the pattern.

99, 92, 85,

_____,

_____,

_____

Deanna has 4 packs of crayons with 8 crayons in each pack. How many crayons does Deanna have in all?

_____

Round each number to the nearest 10. Then, subtract.

979 – 354 is about

_____

**Day 2**

10 ÷ _____ = 2

_____ ÷ 7 = 2

7 × 9 = _____

How many inches long is the worm?

_____

3

3        3

3

Draw square units to show the area of the rectangle.

A = _____ sq. units

Complete the related multiplication facts.

28 ÷ 7        7 × _____

12 ÷ 4        4 × _____

18 ÷ 2        2 × _____

3 in.

4 in.

1 in.

What is the perimeter of this shape?

_____

**Day 3**

3 × 9 = 27

Write a related multiplication sentence.

_____

456 + 327 =

Isabelle wants to cut string to make bracelets. She has 21 inches of string. How many 7-inch pieces of string can she make?

_____

**Day 4**

967 – 794 =

50 × 1 = _____

70 × 9 = _____

80 × 8 = _____

A dump truck can hold about

A. 1 liter of water.
B. 10 liters of water.
C. 1,000 liters of water.

Favorite Pets

How many children voted in all?

_____

Brittany parks her car at 3:30. She puts enough money in the parking meter to go to the mall for 60 minutes. What time should she be back at her car?

_____

1.

4

3            3

4

Draw square units to show the area of the rectangle.

A = _____ sq. units

2.

2 cm

3 cm

3 cm

2 cm

3 cm

What is the perimeter of this shape?

_____

3. A butterfly weighs about

    A. 100 grams.
    B. 1 gram.
    C. 10 grams.

4. Jose parks at 5:20. He only has two quarters to put in the parking meter which will pay for 30 minutes each. What time should he be back at his car?

_____

5. Write the missing numbers to complete the pattern.

204, 208, 212, _____, _____, _____

6. Round each number to the nearest 10. Then, subtract

547 – 265 is about _____

7. 4 × 7 = 28

Write a related multiplication sentence.

_____

8. Vince has 6 bags of marbles. Each bag holds 5 marbles. How many marbles does Vince have in all?

_____

9. 5 × _____ = 40

_____ × 6 = 12

24 ÷ _____ = 8

10. 982 – 398 =

3.OA.3, 3.OA.4, 3.OA.5, 3.OA.9, 3.NBT.1, 3.NBT.2, 3.MD.1, 3.MD.2, 3.MD.5, 3.MD.7, 3.MD.8 CD-104592 • © Carson-Dellosa

## Day 1

Graham wants to tile the kitchen floor. How many 1-foot square tiles will he need to buy?

_____

5 ft.

5 ft.

Complete the table.

| Divide by 2 | |
|---|---|
| 6 | 3 |
| 8 | |
| 10 | |
| 12 | |
| 14 | |

Write <, >, or = to make the statement true.

⬚⬚ (=) ⬚⬚

Complete the related multiplication facts.

$40 \div 8$      $8 \times$ _____

$27 \div 9$      $9 \times$ _____

$6 \div 6$      $6 \times$ _____

## Day 2

4 in.

4 in.

What is the perimeter of this shape?

_____

_____ $\times 3 = 15$

$7 \times$ _____ $= 21$

$30 \div 6 =$ _____

Emily has 10 kittens. She has 2 dishes for the kittens' food. How many kittens will eat at a dish so that there is an equal number at each dish?

_____

Mr. Gupta's class collected 371 canned goods for the food drive. Ms. Dolby's and Mr. Nez's class collected 314 cans each. How many canned goods did all 3 classes collect?

_____

## Day 3

Jason gets up at 7:00. He takes 15 minutes to shower, 5 minutes to brush his teeth, and 20 minutes to eat breakfast. What time is Jason ready to go to school?

_____

Write <, >, or = to make the statement true.

$\frac{4}{4}$ (>) $\frac{1}{4}$

Use the information below to fill in the line plot.

$10\frac{1}{4}$ in. = 3

$10\frac{1}{2}$ in. = 8

$11\frac{1}{4}$ in. = 1

Snakes at the Zoo

$\begin{array}{ccccc} | & | & | & | & | \\ 10\frac{1}{4} & 10\frac{1}{2} & 10\frac{3}{4} & 11 & 11\frac{1}{4} \end{array}$

$90 \times 1 =$ _____

$90 \times 6 =$ _____

$80 \times 9 =$ _____

## Day 4

A juice bottle can hold about

A.  2 liters.
B.  200 liters.
C.  2,000 liters.
D.  20,000 liters.

At the farmers market, Jordan sold 9 pounds of peaches every hour. How many pounds of peaches did Jordan sell during an 8-hour workday?

_____

Divide the number line into eighths.

$\overset{|}{\underset{0}{\longleftarrow}} \qquad\qquad \overset{|}{\underset{1}{\longrightarrow}}$

Label the fractions $\frac{2}{8}$ and $\frac{6}{8}$ on the number line.

Name_____

1. Complete the related multiplication facts.

   $63 \div 9$    $9 \times$ _____

   $24 \div 3$    $3 \times$ _____

   $10 \div 5$    $5 \times$ _____

2. Adrian raked 703 leaves. Alvin raked 217 leaves and added them to Adrian's pile. A large wind blew away 68 of the leaves. How many leaves are left?

   _____

3. $80 \times 1 =$ _____

   $90 \times 4 =$ _____

   $90 \times 8 =$ _____

4. Write <, >, or = to make the statement true.

5. Clarissa wants to put tiles on her closet floor. How many 1-foot square tiles will she need to buy?

   _____

   6 ft.

   2 ft. [        ] 2 ft.

   6 ft.

6.    7 cm      7 cm

   7 cm            7 cm

      7 cm   7 cm

   What is the perimeter of this shape?

   _____

7. Iman gets to the gym at 5:15. He runs on the treadmill for 30 minutes, lifts weights for 15 minutes, and swims in the pool for 20 minutes. What time is Iman ready to leave the gym?

   _____

8. A bird can weigh about

   A.  4 grams.
   B.  40 grams.
   C.  400 grams.
   D.  4,000 grams.

9. Divide the number line into sixths.

10. Label the fractions $\frac{3}{6}$ and $\frac{4}{6}$.

   |←———————————————————|
   0                    1

 3.OA.6, 3.OA.8, 3.NBT.3, 3.NF.2, 3.NF.3, 3.MD.1, 3.MD.2, 3.MD.7, 3.MD.8   CD-104592 • © Carson-Dellosa

**Day 1**

Write <, >, or = to make the statement true.

At 10:35, Sasha started watching a trapdoor spider. She watched for 43 minutes until it caught an insect. What time did it catch an insect?

_____

Matt has 28 baseball cards to give to 7 friends. If he gives the same number to each friend, how many cards will each friend get?

_____

Flowers in My Garden

✱ = 2 flowers

How many flowers are in the garden in total?

_____

**Day 2**

254 + 347 =

Blake is fencing a rectangular dog pen. Two of the sides are 67 feet, and the other two sides are 41 feet. How many feet of fencing will Blake need?

_____

Jennifer jumped over 9 rocks. She jumped over each rock 9 times. How many times did she jump?

_____

Complete the related multiplication facts.

8 ÷ 4        4 × _____

12 ÷ 3        3 × _____

72 ÷ 9        9 × _____

**Day 3**

982 – 398 =

Michelle and Madison are painting an area that is 12 feet by 8 feet. How many square feet do Michelle and Madison have to paint?

_____

_____ × 7 = 7

4 × _____ = 20

16 ÷ 4 = _____

Complete the table.

| Divide by 3 | |
| --- | --- |
| 9 | 3 |
| 21 | |
| 18 | |
| 24 | |
| 12 | |

**Day 4**

Round each number to the nearest 100. Then, subtract.

293 – 187 is about

_____

Kyle has 48 grams of cheese in a bag. Maria has 72 grams of cheese in a bag. How many grams of cheese do Kyle and Maria have altogether?

_____

Shade the circle to show the fraction $\frac{6}{6}$.

Circle all of the shapes with right angles.

1. Warren used a forklift to move 72 plants in the store. He could only fit 8 plants at a time on the forklift. How many trips did he make?

   _____

2. _____ ÷ 2 = 9

   64 ÷ _____ = 8

   4 × 4 = _____

3. Write <, >, or = to make the statement true.

4. 349 + 493 =

5. Round each number to the nearest 100. Then, add.

   349 + 493 is about _____

6. Complete the related multiplication facts.

   8 ÷ 2      2 × _____

   36 ÷ 6      6 × _____

   9 ÷ 9      9 × _____

7. Starting at 11:48, Robert followed a chameleon for 33 minutes. It changed color twice in that time. What time did he stop watching?

   _____

8. Anna is buying trim to go around her rug. Her rug measures 54 inches by 42 inches. How many inches of trim will Anna need to buy?

   _____

9. Jared is repairing 2 windows. The first window measures 12 inches by 8 inches. The second window measures 11 inches by 6 inches. How many square inches of glass will Jared need in all?

   _____

10. Riley weighs 66 kilograms and Xander weighs 84 kilograms. How many more kilograms does Xander weigh than Riley?

    _____

3.OA.3, 3.OA.4, 3.OA.6, 3.NBT.1, 3.NBT.2, 3.NF.3, 3.MD.1, 3.MD.2, 3.MD.7, 3.MD.8     CD-104592 • © Carson-Dellosa

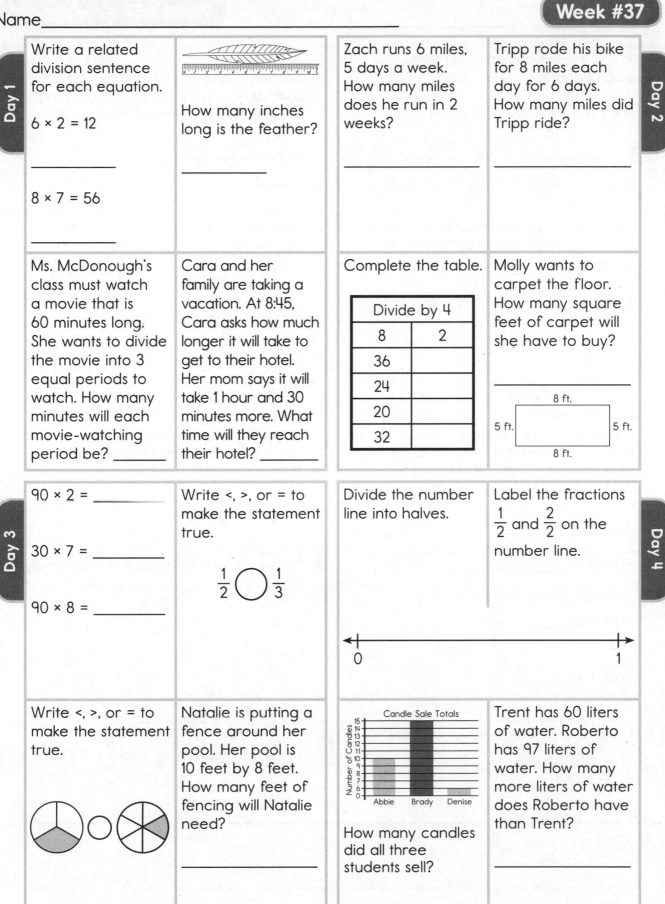

**Day 1**

Write a related division sentence for each equation.

$6 \times 2 = 12$

_____

$8 \times 7 = 56$

_____

How many inches long is the feather?

_____

Ms. McDonough's class must watch a movie that is 60 minutes long. She wants to divide the movie into 3 equal periods to watch. How many minutes will each movie-watching period be? _____

Cara and her family are taking a vacation. At 8:45, Cara asks how much longer it will take to get to their hotel. Her mom says it will take 1 hour and 30 minutes more. What time will they reach their hotel? _____

**Day 2**

Zach runs 6 miles, 5 days a week. How many miles does he run in 2 weeks?

_____

Tripp rode his bike for 8 miles each day for 6 days. How many miles did Tripp ride?

_____

Complete the table.

| Divide by 4 | |
|---|---|
| 8 | 2 |
| 36 | |
| 24 | |
| 20 | |
| 32 | |

Molly wants to carpet the floor. How many square feet of carpet will she have to buy?

_____

8 ft.

5 ft.          5 ft.

8 ft.

**Day 3**

$90 \times 2 =$ _____

$30 \times 7 =$ _____

$90 \times 8 =$ _____

Write <, >, or = to make the statement true.

$\frac{1}{2} \bigcirc \frac{1}{3}$

Divide the number line into halves.

Label the fractions $\frac{1}{2}$ and $\frac{2}{2}$ on the number line.

**Day 4**

0                              1

Write <, >, or = to make the statement true.

Natalie is putting a fence around her pool. Her pool is 10 feet by 8 feet. How many feet of fencing will Natalie need?

_____

Candle Sale Totals

Number of Candles

15 14 13 12 11 10 9 8 7 6 5 4 3 2 1 0

Abbie   Brady   Denise

How many candles did all three students sell?

_____

Trent has 60 liters of water. Roberto has 97 liters of water. How many more liters of water does Roberto have than Trent?

_____

Name_____

1. Write a related division sentence for each equation.

   $9 \times 7 = 63$          $1 \times 9 = 9$

   _____      _____

2. Eight children went for a hike. Each child carried a backpack with 6 bandages in it. Arianna used 2 bandages. How many bandages do the children have left?

   _____

3. Jack set his alarm clock for 7:15 in the morning. He overslept by 30 minutes. What time did Jack wake up?

   _____

4. Kevin wants to tile his bathroom floor. How many 1-foot square tiles will he need?

   _____

   6 ft.
   6 ft.   6 ft.
   6 ft.

5. Uma and Rebecca are sewing trim around their blankets. Uma's blanket measures 36 inches by 30 inches. Rebecca's blanket measures 42 inches by 28 inches. Who will need to buy more trim and how much more trim will she need?

   _____

6. Shauna and Rachel are going on a trip. Shauna's suitcase weighs 11 kilograms. Rachel's suitcase weighs 7 kilograms. How many more kilograms does Shauna's suitcase weigh than Rachel's?

   _____

7. $90 \times 5 =$ _____

   $60 \times 6 =$ _____

   $90 \times 7 =$ _____

8. Write <, >, or = to make the statement true.

   $\frac{1}{8} \bigcirc \frac{1}{6}$

9. Divide the number line into eighths.

10. Label the fractions $\frac{7}{8}$ and $\frac{8}{8}$.

0 |——————————————| 1

 3.OA.5, 3.OA.8, 3.NBT.3, 3.NF.2, 3.NF.3, 3.MD.1, 3.MD.2, 3.MD.7, 3.MD.8   CD-104592 • © Carson-Dellosa

**Day 1**

Jeff read 3 books. Each book had 24 pages. How many pages did Jeff read?

_____

_____ × 7 = 35

9 × _____ = 72

12 ÷ 3 = _____

**Day 2**

Write the missing numbers to complete the pattern.
185, 210, 235,

_____,

_____,

_____

Complete the related multiplication facts.

14 ÷ 7       7 × _____

81 ÷ 9       9 × _____

6 ÷ 2       2 × _____

Maddie's pet bird weighed 45 grams. Lauren's pet bird weighed 52 grams. If Maddie and Lauren put both of their birds on a scale, what would be their combined weight?

_____

Divide the figure into eighths and label each piece with the appropriate fraction.

Draw square units to find the area of the rectangle.

8
4       4
8

A =_____ sq. units

238 + 348 =

**Day 3**

90 × 9 = _____

70 × 4 = _____

40 × 8 = _____

Round each number to the nearest 10. Then, subtract.

765 – 428 is about

_____

**Day 4**

Are these fractions equivalent? _____

Write the fraction shown.

_____

Ava gets to work at 8:32. She has a 20-minute phone call, and then, she checks her email for 15 minutes. Next, she has a 30-minute meeting. What time is it now?

_____

845 – 566 =

Gavin was at the amusement park with 11 friends. On one ride, 2 people can ride in a seat. How many seats did Gavin and his friends sit in?

_____

The third grade classroom has a perimeter of 130 feet. If it is 25 feet wide, how many feet long is the classroom?

_____

Name_____

---

1. Round each number to the nearest 10. Then, subtract

   824 – 548 is about _____

2. _____ ÷ 7 = 3

   45 ÷ _____ = 5

   5 × 4 = _____

---

3. Complete the related multiplication facts.

   8 ÷ 1      1 × _____

   72 ÷ 8     8 × _____

   3 ÷ 3      3 × _____

4. Shade the figure to show $\frac{5}{6}$.

---

5. Liza drank 2 liters of water on Monday, 2 liters of water on Tuesday, and 1 liter of water on Wednesday. How many liters of water did Liza drink on Monday, Tuesday, and Wednesday altogether?

   _____

6. Draw square units to find the area of the rectangle.

   A =_____ sq. units

   7
   6        6
   7

---

7. Adam gets home from school at 3:07. It takes him 20 minutes to eat a snack. Then, he watches TV for 30 minutes. Next, he does his homework for 45 minutes. What time is it when Adam finishes his homework?

   _____

8. Mr. Davidson is building a fence around his backyard, which is a triangle with a perimeter of 198 feet. One side of his backyard is 67 feet. Another side is 47 feet. How many feet long is the third side of his backyard?

   _____

---

9. Divide the figure into sixths and label each piece with the appropriate fraction.

10. 349 + 233 =

---

3.OA.4, 3.OA.6, 3.OA.8, 3.NBT.1, 3.NBT.2, 3.NF.1, 3.MD.1, 3.MD.2, 3.MD.7, 3.MD.8, 3.G.2 CD-104592 • © Carson-Dellosa

**Day 1**

Melinda's desk is a trapezoid that has a perimeter of 120 inches, with two diagonal sides that are 24 inches long, and one base that is 39 inches long. How many inches long is the other base? _____

Write the missing numbers to complete the pattern.
500, 475, 450,
_____,

_____,

**Day 2**

Ava worked on her science project last weekend from 11:45 am to 2:00 pm. How long did Ava work on her project?

_____

Are these fractions equivalent?

_____

---

Banks received a small bag of jellybeans as a gift. There are 63 jellybeans in the bag. He wants to share them equally among 7 people. How many will each person get?

_____

$6 \times 4 \times 2 =$

Malia has 2 trading card books. Each book has 50 cards in it. How many trading cards does Malia have?

_____

$659 - 478 =$

---

**Day 3**

Sierra's family's dog weighs 30 kilograms. Her family's cat weighs 6 kilograms. How many more kilograms does the dog weigh than the cat?

_____

Complete the related multiplication facts.

$14 \div 2$      $2 \times$ _____

$6 \div 3$      $3 \times$ _____

$8 \div 8$      $8 \times$ _____

**Day 4**

What is the total area of this figure?

_____

$20 \times 5 =$ _____

$40 \times 3 =$ _____

$80 \times 4 =$ _____

---

Adrienne had 35 pieces of candy to give away to 5 friends. Ms. Santos then gave each friend 4 more pieces. How many pieces of candy does each friend have?

_____

$955 + 34 =$

Divide the number line into eighths.

Label the fractions $\frac{1}{8}$ and $\frac{5}{8}$.

Name_____

1. Anton has 5 packs of 6 balloons. If he wants to share all of the balloons with 3 friends, how many balloons will each friend get?

   _____

2. 725 – 469 =

3. Write the missing numbers to complete the pattern.

   252, 264, 276, _____, _____, _____

4. Are these fractions equivalent?

   _____

5. 70 × 7 = _____

   50 × 8 = _____

   60 × 3 = _____

6. Divide the number line into sixths. Label the fraction $\frac{2}{6}$.

7. The dimensions of Raul's beach towel are 152 cm by 76 cm. How many centimeters is its perimeter?

   _____

8. Nathan worked on his science project from 8:15 am to 10:30 am and then again from 1:00 pm to 2:30 pm. How long did Nathan work on his science project?

   _____

9. Each box of paper clips weighs 15 grams. If there are 5 boxes of paper clips, how many grams do the boxes weigh together?

   _____

10. What is the total area of this figure?

   _____

 3.OA.3, 3.OA.8, 3.OA.9, 3.NBT.2, 3.NBT.3, 3.NF.2, 3.NF.3, 3.MD.1, 3.MD.2, 3.MD.7, 3.MD.8   CD-104592 • © Carson-Dellosa

Name_____

## Day 1

_____ × 2 = 12

3 × _____ = 12

36 ÷ _____ = 6

Ansley has 2 bird baths in her back yard. Each bird bath holds 2 liters of water. How many liters of water do her bird baths hold in total?

_____

How many inches long is the feather?

_____

$493 + 327 =$

## Day 2

Write the missing numbers to complete the pattern.
615, 605, 595,

_____ ,

_____ ,

_____

What is the total area for this figure? _____

Five spiders are building webs in the barn. How many spider legs are there in all?

_____

$536 - 258 =$

## Day 3

Round each number to the nearest 10. Then, subtract.

578 – 396 is about

_____

A square has one side that measures 6 inches. How many inches is the perimeter of the square?

_____

Renee is making 5 mini pizzas. She has 25 pieces of pepperoni to divide between the pizzas. How many pieces of pepperoni should go on each pizza?

_____

Write the fraction.

_____

## Day 4

Round each number to the nearest 100. Then, add.

588 + 294 is about

_____

Bill is excited to get to the amusement park. His family reaches the amusement park at 8:00. They wait in line to get in for 50 minutes. What time is it when they go inside the park?

_____

Kennedy popped 24 cups of popcorn in 3 days. If she popped the same number of cups each day, how many cups did she pop each day?

_____

Are these fractions equivalent?

_____

© Carson-Dellosa • CD-104592

1. Brantley carries 3 water bottles to football practice. Each water bottle holds 1 liter of water. How many liters of water does Brantley take to football practice?

_____

2. What is the total area for this figure?

_____

3
5
1
9

3. An equilateral triangle has one side that measures 9 cm. How many centimeters is the perimeter of the triangle?

_____

4. The baseball game begins at 7:05. The game takes 2 hours and 45 minutes to play. What time is the baseball game over?

_____

5. $18 \div$ _____ $= 3$

_____ $\div 7 = 9$

$6 \times$ _____ $= 30$

6. Compete the table.

| Divide by 5 | |
|---|---|
| 10 | 2 |
| 30 | |
| 15 | |
| 40 | |
| 45 | |

7. Round each number to the nearest 10. Then, subtract.

557 − 278 is about _____

8. $455 - 347 =$

9.

How many inches long is the toothbrush?

_____

10. Are these fractions equivalent?

_____

 3.OA.4, 3.OA.9, 3.NBT.1, 3.NBT.2, 3.NF.3, 3.MD.1, 3.MD.2, 3.MD.4, 3.MD.7, 3.MD.8   CD-104592 • © Carson-Dellosa

# Answer Key

## Page 9
**Day 1:** 172; 97 pages; 3:30; 13;
**Day 2:** 131; 10, 20, 30; 20 students; 133;
**Day 3:** 7 sausage pizzas; 300, 600, 300;
Check students' answers; 533; **Day 4:** 84;
443; 10, 12, 14; 50 books

## Page 10
1. 20, 30, 50; 2. 11:00; 3. 3; 4. 169; 5. 12 + 15 +
9 = 36 days; 6. 16, 18, 20; 7. dogs; 8. Check
students' answers; 9. 200, 100, 300; 10. 749

## Page 11
**Day 1:** 600, 300, 500; 139; pentagon;
96 cents; **Day 2:** 6:10; 136; 23 push-ups;
439; **Day 3:** 7, 12, 20; 54; 132; 24 peanuts;
**Day 4:** 35 books; 56; C; 30, 50, 50

## Page 12
1. 67, 57, 62; 2. 112; 3. 35; 4. 20, 30, 60;
5. 3:15; 6. 10 students; 7. square; 8.
263 books; 9. 72 hot fudge sundaes; 10.
200, 400, 600

## Page 13
**Day 1:** 8:15; 289; 500 + 40 + 8; 67, 23;
**Day 2:** 14; 12, 5, 11; 420, 425, 430; 40, 70,
80; **Day 3:** hexagon; 4, 8, 2; 359 miles; 700,
400, 900; **Day 4:** 157 books; $1.78; odd; 902

## Page 14
1. 7:15; 2. 11 pages; 3. 500, 200, 600; 4. right
triangle; 5. pine; 6. 80, 20, 70; 7. 14, 23, 17;
8. 676; 9. 641; 10. 101

## Page 15
**Day 1:** 33 pages; 30; $\frac{1}{4}$; Check students'
answers; **Day 2:** 4, 10, 2; 400, 700, 800; 33;
15 people; **Day 3:** 40, 20, 20; 20 flags;

; 289; **Day 4:** 7:45; eight hundred, two
hundred thirty; thirds; 770

## Page 16
1. 965; 2. 116; 3. 11:25; 4. 71, 63; 5. 40, 60, 10;
6. rectangle; 7. 4 students; 8. 6 pounds;

9. 300, 300, 300; 10.

## Page 17
**Day 1:** 54, 34, 64; $\frac{1}{3}$; 170; 146 feet;
**Day 2:** 220 sit-ups; 12 books; 624; 931;
**Day 3:** 5:42; thirds; 45 students; 628;
**Day 4:** 600; 12, 18, 21; 7 ones; square

## Page 18
1. trapezoid; 2. 91, 86, 94; 3. 4:13; 4. 923;
5. 628; 6. 900; 7. 129 balloons; 8. 60; 9. 260;
10. 94, 100, 106

## Page 19
**Day 1:** rectangle or parallelogram;
10, 15, 16; $4.90; 774 pieces; **Day 2:** 890;
563; Check students' arrays; 14 students;
**Day 3:** 209; >, <, =; 794, 994; 75, 78, 81; **Day
4:** 8:22; 8 cm; halves; 190

## Page 20
1. 35, 42, 49; 2. 880; 3. 211; 4. 850;
5. 16 people; 6. 300 cookies; 7. 5:30;
8. cube; 9. 800; 10. 91, 163

## Page 21
**Day 1:** 7:18; 259; 440, 711, 331; 389; **Day 2:** 15,
11, 3; even; 63, 35; 4 cars; **Day 3:** 800;
62 pencils; 573; 41 angelfish; **Day 4:** 601;
110; 8 students; circle

## Page 22
1. reading and music; 2. 18 pieces;
3. 120, 180, 160; 4. 6:47; 5. 400; 6. 996;
7. 189; 8. Check students' answers; 9. 120;
10. 224 shrimp

© Carson-Dellosa • CD-104592

## Page 23
**Day 1:** 4 trees; 150 people; 722; 920;
**Day 2:** 650 people; 62; two hundred twelve; 800; **Day 3:** 154, 157, 160; <, =, <; 227; 154 miles; **Day 4:** 8:36; 20 pictures; 80 or 8 tens; Check students' answers.

## Page 24
1. Check students' answers; 2. 6 erasers; 3. 636; 4. 58; 5. 12:06; 6. 216, 220, 224; 7. 770; 8. 400; 9. about 10; 10. 5 students

## Page 25
**Day 1:** 642; 900; 693, 542, 102; 52 letters; **Day 2:** 59; Check students' answers; 7 inches; 193, 199, 205; **Day 3:** 440 seats; $2.50; 723; 690; **Day 4:** ; 8, 2, 10; 778, 878, 978; 50 people

## Page 26
1. 20 wins; 2. 578, 583, 588; 3. ; 4. 37 items; 5. 582; 6. 164; 7. Check students' answers; 8. 34 bologna sandwiches; 9. 24 ribbons; 10. 970

## Page 27
**Day 1:** 900; 171 days; ; 556; **Day 2:** 47 items; 672, 251; 92, 101, 110; 209; **Day 3:** 9 cars, 751, 485; 970; 339; **Day 4:** $54; $2.42; Check students' drawings; 43

## Page 28
1. ; 2. 73; 3. 26 times; 4. 800; 5. 375, 300; 6. mountains; 7. 909; 8. Check students' drawings; 9. 410; 10. 35 more

## Page 29
**Day 1:** 4 × 4 = 16 books or 4 + 4 + 4 + 4 = 16 books; 1:06; 629; 0, 16, 12; **Day 2:** 10 swimmers; 259; 510; 10, 20, 30; **Day 3:** 1, 1, 0; 64; 28; 30, 36, 42; **Day 4:** A; 212; Check students' answers; 8, 10, 18

## Page 30
1. 8, 5, 2; 2. 1 ball; 3. 0, 6, 16; 4. C; 5. 40, 50, 60; 6. 23, 26, 29; 7. about 28 days; 8. 965; 9. 89; 10. 2, 0, 4

## Page 31
**Day 1:** 0, 0, 4; 250, 14 miles; 50, 48, 46; **Day 2:** 8 × 2 = 16 wheels; 300; 1:32; 70, 80, 90; **Day 3:** 75 people; 1, 0, 1; 7 × 3 = 21; 81 computers; **Day 4:** B; 368; 3, 0, 2; 12, 9, 1

## Page 32
1. 14 monkeys; 2. 2, 8, 21; 3. 4 × 3 = 12; 4. 24, 12, 4; 5. 20, 50, 80; 6. 56, 53, 50; 7. 3, 2, 0; 8. 7 turtles; 9. 389; 10. 16 hours

## Page 33
**Day 1:** 5 × 3 = 15; 206 pages; 18, 18, 16; 40, 60, 80; **Day 2:** 2, 2, 27; 8:00; 35 cookies; 59, 52; **Day 3:** 32 bags; 110; 8, 6, 21; 3 x 3 = 9; **Day 4:** 6, 8, 10, 12; 100, 120, 140; 965; 18, 9, 16

## Page 34
1. 14, 16, 18; 2. 120, 60, 160; 3. 15 Apple Puffs; 4. 4 × 2 = 8 or 2 × 4 = 8; 5. 9, 1, 9; 6. 3 × 4 = 12; 7. 6, 16, 4; 8. 42 cookies; 9. 5 × 2 = 10; 10. 25 pictures

## Page 35
**Day 1:** 60, 90, 120; 860; 0, 4, 42; 12 feet; **Day 2:** 12, 15, 18; 802; sunny; B; **Day 3:** 3 × 5 = 15; 726; 40 stickers; 20, 24, 18; **Day 4:** 8, 4, 8; 4:52; 34; $4

CD-104592 • © Carson-Dellosa

## Page 36
1. 140, 40, 90; 2. $4; 3. 21, 24, 27; 4. 5, 5, 8;
5. 18 songs; 6. C; 7. 16, 2, 40; 8. 7 × 3 = 21;
9. 400; 10. 10 swimsuits

## Page 37
**Day 1:** 5 × 5; 177; (clock); 8, 12, 16, 20;
**Day 2:** 24 letters; 1 × 6 = 6 or 6 × 1 = 6;
220; 80, 180, 120; **Day 3:** 7, 4, 27; Check
students' answers; $16; 16, 9, 18; **Day 4:**
7 × 6 = 42; 800; 887; 98 beads

## Page 38
1. 18; 2. 3 × 7; 3. 6, 8, 54; 4. 8 × 7 = 56;
5. 210, 160, 200; 6. 24, 28, 32, 36;
7. 25 pieces; 8. 10, 49, 27; 9. 9, 8, 7;
10. 2 × 5 = 10 or 5 × 2 = 10

## Page 39
**Day 1:** 8 stars; 180; 240, 240, 270; 5, 8, 9;
**Day 2:** 1 piece; 415; 21 ÷ 3 = 7; 15, 20, 25,
30; **Day 3:** 4, 15, 7; 9:18; 7 players; 28, 63,
40; **Day 4:** 6 × 5 = 30 or 5 × 6 = 30;
100, 120, 180; 5, 9, 5; 22

## Page 40
1. 3, 8, 2; 2. 7 × 3 = 21 or 3 × 7 = 21;
3. 4, 4, 3; 4. 2 fumbles; 5. 7 sets; 6. 35, 40,
45; 7. 90, 80, 200; 8. 8; 9. 3 fans;
10. 64, 35, 6

## Page 41
**Day 1:** 150, 240, 200; 24 gingerbread men;
732; 6, 56, 7; **Day 2:** 18, 24, 30, 36; 2, 12, 45;
308; 7 pins; **Day 3:** 4 × 7 = 28 or 7 × 4 = 28;
4 gel pens; 100; 2 circles; **Day 4:** Answers
will vary; 16, 9, 8; 6:22; 6, 8, 8

## Page 42
1. 250, 300, 150; 2. 42, 48, 54;
3. 9 × 6 = 54 or 6 × 9 = 54; 4. Answers will
vary; 5. 8, 3, 7; 6. 5 games; 7. 3 sets;
8. 3, 4, 8; 9. 6 cars; 10. 7, 12, 30

## Page 43
**Day 1:** 9 × 5 = 45 or 5 × 9 = 45; 6 × 3;
11:17; 7 sets; **Day 2:** Answers will vary;
450; 14, 48, 32; 8 towels; **Day 3:** 35, 6, 4;
596; 3 cupcakes; 360, 250, 420; **Day 4:**
8 pounds; 449; 9, 9, 6; 14, 21, 28, 35

## Page 44
1. 2 × 8 = 16 or 8 × 2 = 16; 2. Answers will
vary; 3. 36, 8, 8; 4. 9 pounds; 5. 5 triangles;
6. 480, 300, 350; 7. 42, 49, 56, 63; 8. 4, 6, 5;
9. 22 stickers; 10. 3, 3, 5 or 3, 5, 3

## Page 45
**Day 1:** 100; 36, 48, 10; 6 players;
9 × 4 = 36 or 4 × 9 = 36; **Day 2:** 2:53;
24 lettuce leaves; 7 pieces of paper;
16, 24, 32, 40; **Day 3:** 33 points; 2 pieces;
9, 24, 6; 280, 240, 400; **Day 4:** 20 seedlings;
434 miles; Answers will vary; 3, 5, 9

## Page 46
1. 8 ounces; 2. 45, 6, 4; 3. Answers will vary;
4. 12; 5. 48, 56, 64, 72; 6. 8 × 7 = 56
or 7 × 8 = 56; 7. 100, 270, 240; 8. 6, 9, 2; 9.
2 models; 10. 48 bags

## Page 47
**Day 1:** 7, 14, 27; 12 flowers; 6 × 9 = 54 or
9 × 6 = 54; 350, 210, 450; **Day 2:** 937;
35 gallons; Answers will vary; 8 clubs;
**Day 3:** 489; 7, 5, 81; 9, 42, 9; 10 pieces;
**Day 4:** $16; 7, 2, 8; 340; 18, 27, 36, 45

**Page 48**

1. 490, 320, 150; 2. 3 buckets; 3. 11 candy bars; 4. 54, 63, 72, 81; 5. 3 × 9 = 27 or 9 × 3 = 27; 6. Answers will vary; 7. 48, 5, 7; 8. 7 pots; 9. 96 times; 10. 3, 6, 16

**Page 49**

**Day 1:** 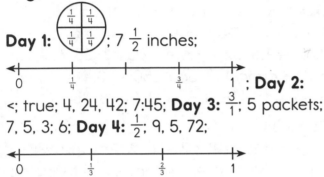 ; $7\frac{1}{2}$ inches;

Day 2: <; true; 4, 24, 42; 7:45; **Day 3:** $\frac{3}{1}$; 5 packets; 7, 5, 3; 6; **Day 4:** $\frac{1}{2}$; 9, 5, 72;

**Page 50**

1. Answers will vary; 2. >; 3. $\frac{6}{1}$; 4. $\frac{1}{3}$; 5. $6\frac{1}{2}$ inches: 6. false; 7. 30, 2, 6; 8. 45 minutes;

9 & 10.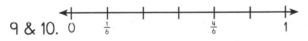

**Page 51**

**Day 1:** $\frac{7}{1}$; 5 times; 775; 4; **Day 2:** 200; 5;

**Day 3:** $5\frac{1}{4}$ inches; 420, 450, 160;

; true;

**Day 4:** or ; 24 tents; 24, 9, 20; <

**Page 52**

1. $\frac{5}{1}$; 2. $7\frac{1}{4}$ inches;

3 & 4.:

5. Answers will vary; 6. 8;

7. ; 8. true; 9. =; 10. 30, 36, 21

**Page 53**

**Day 1:** $\frac{3}{4}$; 24, 48, 96; $1\frac{1}{2}$ inches; 3, 2, 54;

**Day 2:** 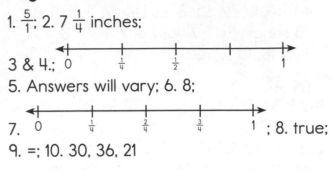 ; 2 miles; 8; 35 minutes; **Day 3:** 19 rubber bands; 5, 6, 15;

;

**Day 4:** Answers will vary; 6, 3; <; true

**Page 54**

1. $\frac{6}{8}$; 2. 12; 3. >; 4. $3\frac{1}{2}$ inches; 5. Answers may vary; 6. false;

7 & 8. 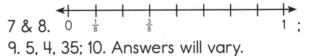 ; 9. 5, 4, 35; 10. Answers will vary.

**Page 55**

**Day 1:** 870; 4; $8\frac{1}{4}$ inches; 4, 2, 9; **Day 2:** 810;

<; ; 42 people; **Day 3:** 560, 320, 560;

yes; ; 5 pictures; **Day 4:** 4 students;

7, 2, 28;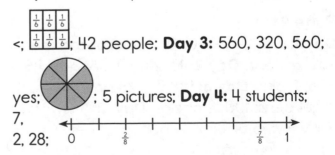

CD-104592 • © Carson-Dellosa

## Page 56

1 and 2.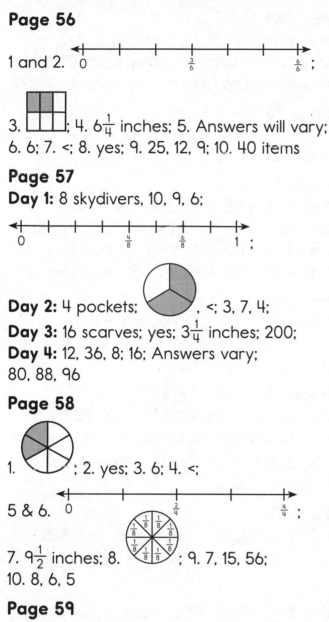

3. ; 4. $6\frac{1}{4}$ inches; 5. Answers will vary;
6. 6; 7. <; 8. yes; 9. 25, 12, 9; 10. 40 items

## Page 57

**Day 1:** 8 skydivers, 10, 9, 6;

**Day 2:** 4 pockets, , <; 3, 7, 4;
**Day 3:** 16 scarves; yes; $3\frac{1}{4}$ inches; 200;
**Day 4:** 12, 36, 8; 16; Answers vary;
80, 88, 96

## Page 58

1. ; 2. yes; 3. 6; 4. <;

5 & 6.

7. $9\frac{1}{2}$ inches; 8. ; 9. 7, 15, 56;
10. 8, 6, 5

## Page 59

**Day 1:** 70, 240, 140; 6; Answers will vary;
4:19; **Day 2:** 983; $1;

**Day 3:** 326; >; $2\frac{1}{2}$ inches; 54 keys;

**Day 4:** yes; $\frac{2}{4} = \frac{4}{8}$ and $\frac{3}{4} = \frac{6}{8}$; Answers will vary; 6, 5, 6

## Page 60

1. 3, 7, 5; 2. 9 packages;

3 & 4.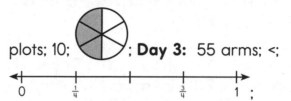
5. Answers will vary; 6. $8\frac{1}{2}$ inches;

7. ; 8. 8; 9. >; 10. $\frac{1}{3} = \frac{2}{6}$ and $\frac{2}{3} = \frac{4}{6}$

## Page 61

**Day 1:** 4, 6, 15; Answers will vary; no; $\frac{1}{2}$ and $\frac{2}{4}$; **Day 2:** 7 seats; Check students' line

plots; 10; ; **Day 3:** 55 arms; <;

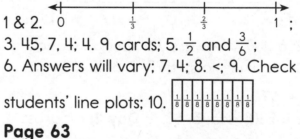

**Day 4:** 8, 4, 4; 12; 11 erasers; 520

## Page 62

1 & 2.
3. 45, 7, 4; 4. 9 cards; 5. $\frac{1}{2}$ and $\frac{3}{6}$;
6. Answers will vary; 7. 4; 8. <; 9. Check

students' line plots; 10.

## Page 63

**Day 1:** Answers will vary; 77, 73, 69; 8, 56,
4; 16; **Day 2:** Answers will vary; $14;

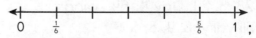

**Day 3:** 40, 360, 60; Check students' line
plots; <; 54 miles; **Day 4:** 300; 5 candies;
no; $\frac{1}{2}$ and $\frac{4}{8}$

**Page 64**

1. <; 2. Check students' line plots; 3. no;

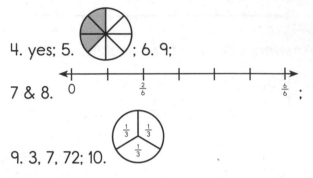

4. yes; 5. ![pie chart shaded]; 6. 9;

7 & 8. ![number line 0 to 6/6 with 2/6 marked];

9. 3, 7, 72; 10. ![circle divided into thirds, each 1/3]

**Page 65**

**Day 1:** 81, 6, 5; 45 spots; >; $\frac{1}{8}$; **Day 2:** no; 791; 39 stickers; Check students' line plots; **Day 3:** 6, 7, 20; 177;

![number line 0 to 1 with 1/8 and 4/8 marked]; **Day 4:** 12; 6 lemon drops; 7, 8, 8; Answers will vary.

**Page 66**

1. yes; 2. $\frac{3}{3}$ ;

3 & 4. ![number line 0 to 1 with 1/6 and 3/6 marked] ;

5. 12; 6. <; 7. Answers will vary; 8. Check students' line plots; 9. 72, 7, 6; 10. 63 miles

**Page 67**

**Day 1:** 1:30; <; $\frac{8}{8}$; 5, 63, 2; **Day 2:** 6 cards; $4\frac{1}{4}$ inches; ![number line 0 to 4/4 with 2/4 marked] ;

**Day 3:** 71 games; Check students' line plots; yes; 28, 8, 24; **Day 4:** 54 swings; Answers will vary; 8; 4, 8, 6

**Page 68**

1. <; 2. 6; 3. $\frac{2}{2}$; 4. Check students' line plots;

5. ![pie chart divided into eighths, each 1/8]; 6. yes; 7. $5\frac{1}{2}$ inches; 8. 2, 3, 1;

9 & 10. ![number line 0 to 1 with 3/8 and 5/8 marked]

**Page 69**

**Day 1:** 2:45; 72, 8, 10; 6 apples; 6, 7, 2; **Day 2:** C; 971; no; 300; **Day 3:** 12; 107; <; $\frac{1}{4}$; **Day 4:** 9 cm; 6 books; 8 toy cars; 82, 77, 72

**Page 70**

1. 7:15; 2. B; 3. 12; 4. 20 cm; 5. 24, 5, 8; 6. 751; 7. 6 books; 8. <; 9. 9 pages; 10. $\frac{6}{8}$

**Page 71**

**Day 1:** 14, 6, 48; 7:35; 340; 126 shells; **Day 2:** 7 × 5 = 35; 16 inches; 5, 64, 9; 751; **Day 3:** 168, 162, 156; B; 177; 28 fish; **Day 4:** 20, 280, 480; 20; 490; 9 pickles

**Page 72**

1. 40, 7, 12; 2. 240, 180, 270; 3. 8 cars; 4. 40 miles; 5. 10:35; 6. 10 inches; 7. B; 8. 14; 9. 20, 32, 9; 10. 12 shells

**Page 73**

**Day 1:** >; 8 pages; ![grid rectangle] 28; 30, 540, 400; **Day 2:** 6, 5, 5; 16 stickers; 20 units; yes; **Day 3:** 974; $\frac{4}{8}$; 5:03; 9, 8, 8; **Day 4:** 289; 9 seeds; C; 8, 2, 2

**Page 74**

1. 993; 2. 193; 3. <; 4. 8, 5, 9; 5. $\frac{3}{6}$; 6. $25; 7. ![grid rectangle] 8; 8. 24 units; 9. 7:15; 10. A

**Page 75**

**Day 1:** 78, 71, 64; 32 crayons; $7\frac{3}{4}$ inches; ![grid rectangle] 9; **Day 2:** 630; 5, 14, 63; 4, 3, 9; 8 inches; **Day 3:** 9 × 3 = 27; 783; 50, 630, 640; C; **Day 4:** 3 pieces; 173; 8 children; 4:30

**Page 76**

1. ![grid rectangle] 12; 2. 13 cm; 3. B; 4. 6:20; 5. 216, 220, 224; 6. 280; 7. 7 × 4 = 28; 8. 30 marbles; 9. 8, 2, 3; 10. 584

CD-104592 • © Carson-Dellosa

## Page 77
**Day 1:** 25 tiles; 4, 5, 6, 7; =; 5, 3, 1; **Day 2:** 16 inches; 5, 3, 5; 5 kittens; 999 cans;
**Day 3:** 7:40; >; Check students' line plots; 90, 540, 720;
**Day 4:** A; 72 pounds;

## Page 78
1. 7, 8, 2; 2. 852 leaves; 3. 80, 360, 720; 4. =; 5. 12 tiles; 6. 42 cm; 7. 6:20; 8. B;

9 & 10.
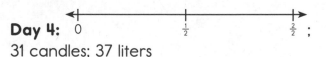

## Page 79
**Day 1:** =; 11:18; 4 cards; 15 flowers;
**Day 2:** 601; 216 feet; 81 times; 2, 4, 8;
**Day 3:** 584; 96 square feet; 1, 5, 4; 7, 6, 8, 4; **Day 4:** 100; 120 grams; ; Check students' answers.

## Page 80
1. 9 trips; 2. 18, 8, 16; 3. =; 4. 842; 5. 800; 6. 4, 6, 1; 7. 12:21; 8. 192 inches; 9. 162 square inches; 10. 18 kilograms

## Page 81
**Day 1:** 12 ÷ 6 = 2 or 12 ÷ 2 = 6, 56 ÷ 8 = 7 or 56 ÷ 7 = 8; $9\frac{3}{4}$ inches; 20 minutes; 10:15;
**Day 2:** 60 miles; 48 miles; 9, 6, 5, 8; 40 square feet; **Day 3:** 180, 210; 720; >; >; 36 feet;

**Day 4:**
0        $\frac{1}{2}$        $\frac{2}{2}$ ;
31 candles; 37 liters

## Page 82
1. 63 ÷ 9 = 7 or 63 ÷ 7 = 9, 9 ÷ 1 = 9 or 9 ÷ 9 =1; 2. 46 bandages; 3. 7:45; 4. 36 tiles; 5. Rebecca, 8 inches; 6. 4 kilograms; 7. 450, 360, 630; 8. <;

9 & 10.
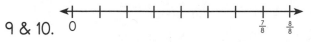

## Page 83
**Day 1:** 72 pages; 5, 8, 4; 97 grams; Answers will vary; **Day 2:** 260, 285, 310; 2, 9, 3;
32; 586; **Day 3:** 810, 280, 320; 340; 9:37; 279; **Day 4:** yes; $\frac{4}{4}$; 6 seats; 40 feet

## Page 84
1. 270; 2. 21, 9, 20; 3. 8, 9, 1; 4. 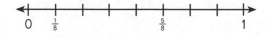;

5. 5 liters; 6. 42; 7. 4:42; 8. 84 feet; 9. Answers will vary; 10. 582

## Page 85
**Day 1:** 33 inches; 425, 400, 375; 9 jellybeans; 48; **Day 2:** 2 hours and 15 minutes; yes; 100 trading cards; 181; **Day 3:** 24 kilograms; 7, 2, 1; 11 pieces of candy; 989; **Day 4:** 48 square units; 100, 120, 320;

0        $\frac{1}{8}$        $\frac{5}{8}$        1

© Carson-Dellosa • CD-104592

## Page 86

1. 10 balloons; 2. 256; 3. 288, 300, 312; 4. yes; 5. 490, 400, 180;

6.

7. 456 cm; 8. 3 hours and 45 minutes or 225 minutes; 9. 75 grams; 10. 20 square units

## Page 87

**Day 1:** 6, 4, 6; 4 liters; $7\frac{1}{4}$ inches; 820; **Day 2:** 585, 575, 565; 41 square units; 40 legs; 278; **Day 3:** 180; 24 inches; 5 pieces; $\frac{2}{8}$; **Day 4:** 900, 8:50; 8 cups; yes

## Page 88

1. 3 liters; 2. 24 square units; 3. 27 centimeters; 4. 9:50; 5. 6, 63, 5; 6. 6, 3, 8, 9; 7. 280; 8. 108; 9. $9\frac{1}{2}$ inches; 10. yes

CD-104592 • © Carson-Dellosa